W9-BIM-466

THE COMPLETE BOOK OF

Decorating Techniques

THE COMPLETE BOOK OF

Decorating Techniques

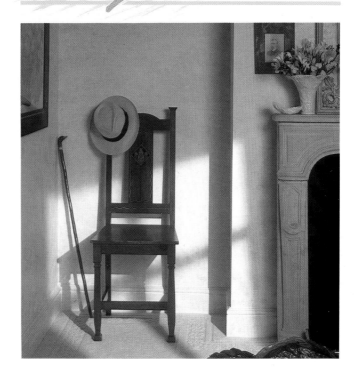

LINDA GRAY
WITH JOCASTA INNES

LITTLE, BROWN AND COMPANY
BOSTON NEW YORK TORONTO LONDON

Copyright © 1986 by Orbis Book Publishing Corporation Limited, Little, Brown
and Company (UK),
Jocasta Innes' text copyright © 1986 by Jocasta Innes

All Rights Reserved. No part of this book may be reproduced in any form or by
any electronic or mechanical means, including information storage and retrieval
systems, without permission in writing from the publisher, except by a reviewer
who may quote brief passages in a review.

ISBN 0-316-32757-3

Library of Congress Cataloging Card No. 86-51234

Printed in Italy

Contents

Introduction

This book is dedicated to all those who have ever thought of decorating their homes and regretfully decided that it was too difficult. It takes you from the basics of painting and papering right through to fashionable paint treatments like simple sponging and ragging plus realistic tortoiseshell and marbling effects which can turn a piece of chipboard into a work of art. There are plenty of room sets to inspire you and every step is illustrated to show just how it's done. Why do it yourself? Because it improves your home and gives you the satisfaction of knowing that the job's well done. It's good, creative fun, saves you money and reflects your tastes and ideas.

Below A glossy white staircase winds upwards and is echoed by ceiling beams in high-sheen white.

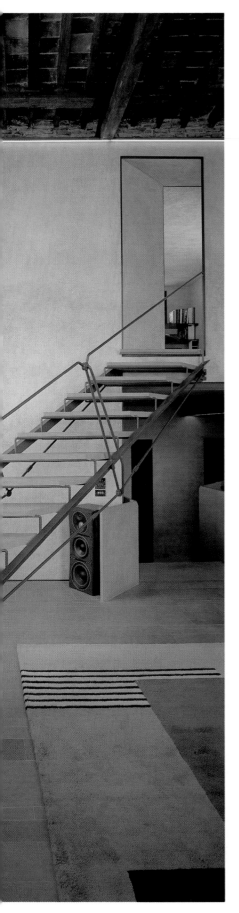

Far left: An avant-garde staircase sets the tone for this monochrome hallway, with stippled walls in subtle grey and a geometric rug for cool sophistication.

Top: This wooden bench, a focal point between a pair of interesting double doors, sits on an immaculate sanded and sealed floor.

Left: Once you have chosen major paint and wallpaper treatments, don't neglect accessories, such as these toning blue-grey vases, which add the finishing touches to a room, giving it character and appeal.

First Steps

Decorating can be fun, but nobody pretends that the preparation is anything but a chore. It's messy, time-consuming and often takes far longer than the decorating itself. Yet it is essential, because paint can't hide a rough surface and new wallpaper may not adhere to old wallpaper, or to greasy walls.

The same principles apply to ceilings too, of course. And make absolutely sure that before you start you have assembled all the essential equipment — nothing could be more irritating than having to break off work and trek to the local home improvement store. Study this chapter carefully and master the techniques — then the fun can begin!

Smoothly finished surfaces create a sophisticated, elegant mood (right), whilst rough-textured walls echo the natural feel of wood and terracotta (below).

If your home is still new you may find that you have only a few cracks to fill in and sand, and that washing down will complete the process, but in an old house there may be layers of wallpaper to remove and defects in plaster to repair. Make the task easier by moving out as much furniture as you can from the room where you plan to work (see below). Shift the rest to the middle of the floor, covering it with old sheets for protection. Remove the curtains and take up carpet if you can, or, if you can't, cover it with a plastic dropcloth plus a sheet to soak up spills. (Don't use newspaper – it moves too easily and has a tendency to leave newsprint.) Take down light fixtures, curtain rails and picture hooks so that the room is as clear as you can make it. Don't forget to cover yourself with jeans and an old shirt (pullovers may leave fluff on fresh paint) and a headscarf if your hair is long. Wear a pair of old sneakers and leave them at the door when you go out so you don't walk paint throughout the house. Before you start, collect all the equipment you need for the day and bring along a

radio and plenty to drink. Decorating is thirsty work and you'll need a supply of soft drinks or milk to minimise the effect of dust and chemicals. Finally, work out a realistic timetable for your project and aim to complete one section at a time. Even if you are tackling a whole house task by task rather than room by room, try to finish one room first so that you have somewhere to sit, or sleep, in relative comfort.

Equipment

You will need:
- a stripping knife or scraper with a wide blade for removing swathes of wallpaper or paint.
- a flexible filling knife for pressing filler into cracks.
- a sanding block (buy one or use a scrap of wood) plus silicon carbide paper which can be used wet or dry – it's more expensive than sandpaper but gives a finer finish.
- a bucket of warm water and liquid detergent for washing down walls and stripping off wallpaper.
- a large sponge.
- a wire brush for scoring the

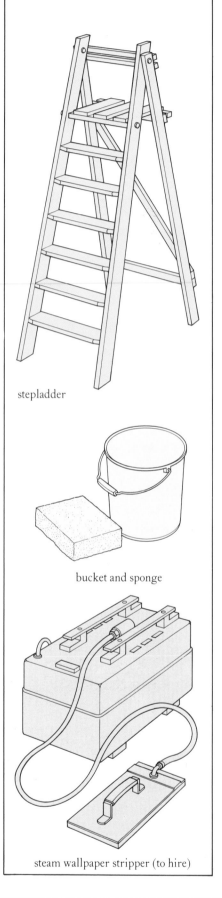

stepladder

bucket and sponge

steam wallpaper stripper (to hire)

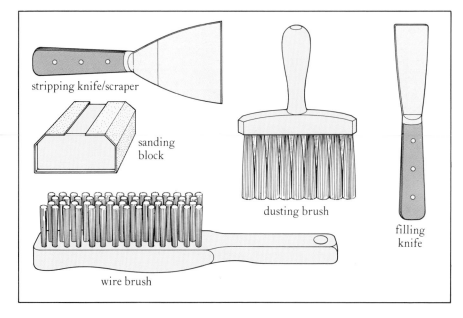

stripping knife/scraper

sanding block

dusting brush

filling knife

wire brush

For awkward areas like stairwells safe access is all-important.

Stairs with a quarter landing: you'll need a full-size ladder at the bottom of the stairs plus stepstools and two planks arranged in an L-shape. Nail a board to the quarter landing to keep the steps in place and nail the planks together, and to the stepstool, for complete safety. Tie some padding around the top of the ladder and the stepstool so that they don't mark the walls.

Stairs with a half landing: nail two boards to the floor of the turn to support two ladders facing each other and lash a plank securely from one to the other.

Ban everyone from the area while work is in progress!

A straight stairway: rent a scaffold with adjustable feet and a wide platform.

surface of stubborn wallcoverings to allow the water to penetrate.
● a dusting brush to remove debris from the wall surface.
● a stepladder with a firm platform.

● a steam stripper if you are tackling a large area or removing several layers of old wallpaper.
● full-size ladders, planks and a stepstool if you are decorating awkward areas like stairwells.

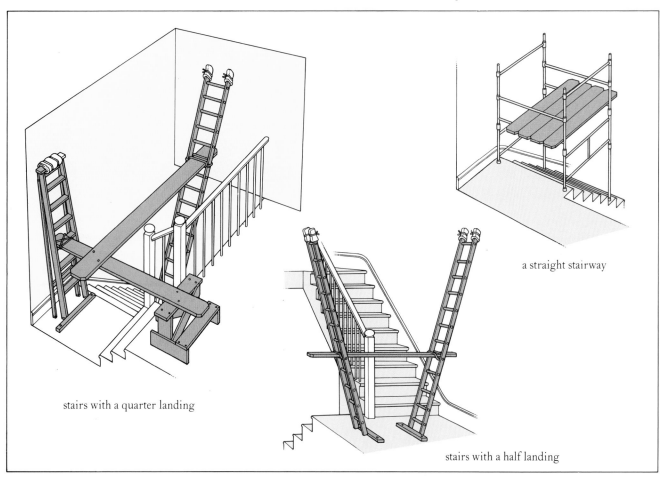

stairs with a quarter landing

a straight stairway

stairs with a half landing

Stripping Wallpaper

Always remove old wallpaper before redecorating if:

. . . there are already several layers on the wall.

. . . the wallpaper is peeling in several places.

. . . the color is dark and likely to bleed.

. . . it has an impermeable surface.

. . . it is affected by damp.

Remember that any flaws, bumps or seams will show through if you paint or paper on top of existing wall-covering. In addition, the weight of the new paper or paint may pull it away from the wall. That's why it's nearly always better to remove wall-paper before you redecorate, however unappealing the prospect may be.

To remove wallpaper, first run your hand over it to assess its type. If it has a glazed or water-resistant finish, if it's made from vinyl or is a special wallcovering like burlap or grasscloth, try peeling it away at the baseboard level corner. These wall-coverings often have a paper back-ing designed to remain on the wall while the top strips smoothly away. If this is in good condition, use it as a lining, if you are redecorating with paint or a heavy wallcovering. Remove the backing if you plan to use a light wallpaper (because the seams may show through), or if it is on top of another layer of wallpaper, or if it does not adhere closely to the wall.

Ordinary wallpaper is unlikely to peel away so easily but as it is absorbent it can be removed with water. Soak plaster walls with a solution of household detergent and water applied with a sponge. Work from the top down so that the water runs over the wallpaper. (Although you should avoid overwetting, for safety, turn off the electricity at the mains before you douse the area around sockets and light switches.) In theory, you should not use water when stripping plasterboard as it

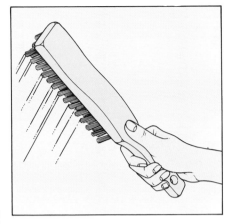

1

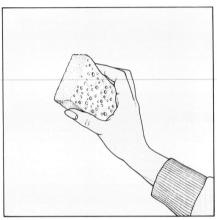

2

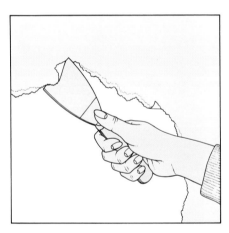

3

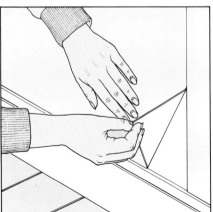

Stripping wallpaper

To strip wallpaper, especially if it has been overpainted or has a washable finish, score its surface with a wire brush. This will help the water to penetrate the paper more easily.

Make a solution of household detergent and water and sponge it over the wallpaper, working from the top of the wall down. Don't forget to switch off the electricity at the mains when you tackle patches around sockets and light switches.

Once the wallpaper is soaked thoroughly, strip it off using a scraper with a wide blade. Work carefully to avoid making any chips in the plaster, as this will only mean extra work later.

Stripping vinyl

For glazed, water-resistant or vinyl wallpapers which often have a paper backing, carefully peel away the top layer starting at the baseboard level corner. If the backing is in good condition, you can use it as a basis for paint or a heavy wallcovering.

may cause the core to swell, but in practice it is often impossible to remove wallpaper any other way. Use the minimum of water and go easy with the scraper as the board is easily punctured. Whatever the surface, work steadily and carefully; any chips you make in the wall will have to be filled in later.

If wallpaper has been over-painted or has a washable finish it may resist the sponge and water method. Score the surface with a wire brush to allow the water to penetrate and leave it to soak for a while before you attempt to remove it with a scraper.

It may be worth renting a steam wallpaper stripper if you have a large area to deal with or several layers of wallpaper to remove. Fill the machine with water and, when it is ready, press the steaming plate to the wall with one hand while you strip the wallpaper with the other (see below).

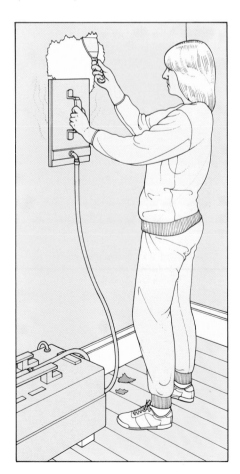

Stripping Paint

Usually all you need to do before redecorating painted walls is to wash down, using a solution of household detergent, and then rinse with water. The exceptions are:

. . . solvent- or oil-based paints, which should be finely sanded so the new layer of paint will adhere to the wall.

. . . a flawed surface. Lift off flaking paint with a scraper and sand down. Similarly, sand any runs or sags in existing paintwork to produce a uniform finish. Apply a coat of stabilising primer to prevent any further flaking.

. . . distemper and whitewash. You'll know immediately if these have been used (though they are rarely applied today) because they wash off the wall, leaving a creamy residue on your cloth or sponge. New paint will not adhere to distemper or whitewash: to remove it, use a stiff brush and plain water, which should be renewed when it becomes milky. Finish by washing with detergent solution to banish the final traces. If you can't remove it completely then apply a coat of oil-based primer/sealer before repainting.

Remedial Work

Once you've stripped off the old wallpaper and removed flaking paint, take a look at the condition of the walls. Now's the time to deal with any underlying problems so you can prepare a smooth surface for redecoration.

Mould

Is the mould caused by penetrating damp from the outside, rising damp which has bypassed a faulty or non-existent vapor barrier or by condensation? The easiest way to find out is to dry the damp patch temporarily with a hair dryer or fan heater, then stick aluminium foil over the affected area with adhesive tape, making sure that the edges are

completely sealed. Leave for one week, then examine the results. If there are drops of moisture on the surface of the foil, the problem is caused by condensation. If the foil is dry on the outside and damp on the underside, you have rising or penetrating damp.

Whatever the cause, the problem must be tackled at source. This may involve quite a bit of inconvenience, but untreated damp will ruin new decor and may ultimately affect the structure of your house.

Penetrating damp should be traced – the walls may need to be repointed, gutters repaired and so on. Rising damp means that the vapor barrier needs attention.

Condensation can only be cured by correcting the balance between warmth and ventilation. If this is the problem, install an extractor fan in troublesome areas like kitchens and bathrooms and consider a dehumidifier if your bedrooms or living rooms are affected. Check to make sure that any blocked-in fireplaces have a grille for adequate ventilation.

Once you have dealt with the cause of the damp you can wipe away the mould. Wash with a solution of one part bleach to five parts water. If you're decorating with wallpaper, choose an adhesive containing fungicide. In places where condensation is difficult to control, it may be preferable to use alkyd paint.

Efflorescence

This is the term for the white salts which work their way through new plaster as it dries out. Although it's rarely necessary these days to wait a year for plaster to dry, you may have to delay using wallpaper or solvent-based paints for a few weeks (though you can use latex straight away). If you notice efflorescence, brush it off and then wait a week to see if it recurs. Repeat the process until the salts no longer appear and the walls are dry.

Cracks

These vary in size from hairline cracks to large gaps in the plaster. Fill hairline cracks with a multi-purpose ready-mixed filler (expensive, but you will only need to use a small quantity at a time) or a cellulose filler that you mix with water to the required consistency. Choose a flexible sealant for cracks between walls and door frames or windows where movement is likely. For large-scale repairs you will find that ready-mixed products are uneconomical; buy plaster by the bag as a cheap alternative to a commercial filler.

You may need to open out a small crack before you can pack it with filler. Use the tip of a screwdriver or a putty knife and clean out the dust with a small dampened paintbrush or toothbrush. Apply the filler with a narrow filling knife, leave to dry, and then sand until smooth using a gentle circular movement so that the filling blends into the surrounding wall.

To fill chips at the corners of walls, apply several layers of filler until the level is slightly higher than that of the wall. Allow to dry, and then sand until flush.

To fill holes in plaster, gradually build up layers of filler. First cut back the damaged plaster until you reach the part that's sound, then brush out the loose residue. Use plaster or filler mixed to a stiff, even consistency, and when the final layer is dry, sand level with the wall.

Don't attempt to fill holes wider than about 8 inches in diameter unless you are experienced at plastering. Although modern plasters are easier to apply and quick to dry, plastering a large area is still best left to the skilled amateur or to the trained professional.

After filling, the wall may look patchy but should now present a clean, even surface for redecoration. What if it doesn't? Walls in cottages and houses over 150 years old, for

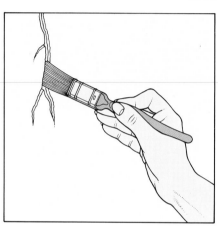

1

2

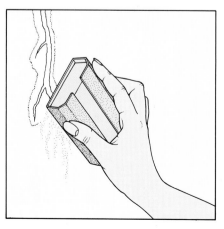

3

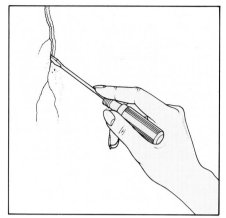

4

Filling cracks

With the top of a screwdriver or putty knife open out any small cracks in the plaster. This makes applying the filler a much less fiddly job.

Dampen a small paintbrush or toothbrush and use it to remove the dust and small particles from inside the crack and the surrounding area.

Apply the filler to the crack with a narrow filling knife, leaving it slightly higher than the wall surface. Wait until the filler has dried out completely before sanding.

Using a sanding block, smooth the filled crack with a gentle circular movement. Sand until the filling is flush and blends into the surrounding wall.

example, are often rough and un-even. Consider the following alternatives:

1. You may have difficulty in papering an irregular surface (choose conventional wallpaper and a small random design if you do) but you can always use one of the paint treatments shown in the second half of the book to add pattern.

2. If you can afford to lose a little space, dry-line the walls using plasterboard mounted on boards. This not only provides an even surface but effectively insulates homes with solid walls. Employ a professional for this purpose.

3. Use a skim of plaster to level out dips in the wall. First coat the wall with stabilising solution. Allow this to dry and then apply skimming plaster with a wide applicator, working in overlapping horizontal bands. When the plaster starts to dry, move the applicator in the opposite direction to remove the

excess. Finish by sanding. As this is a complicated business, you may feel happier employing a professional.

4. Use lining paper, hung horizontally as a base for most wallpapers or vertically if you intend to paint or to hang heavy wallcoverings such as paperbacked burlap.

5. Hang a relief wallcovering intended as a base for paint. This performs a similar function in disguising the rough surface and allows you to select a regular relief pattern or particular motif, rather than the all-over roughness of textured paint.

Although a chore, conscientious preparation is vital, especially if surfaces are simply to be painted.

Ask the Professionals

Q I have just moved to a house where the paint on the walls is flaking badly. What should I do?

A *If the problem is concentrated in specific areas try removing the damaged paint with a scraper and sanding level with the surrounding wall. If it is extensive, it is better to strip solvent-based paint with an electric paint remover, latex with chemical stripper. You need only treat the parts affected, but it is advisable to finish by coating the entire wall with stabilising solution.*

Q I really don't want to remove the existing wallpaper before repainting. What treatment does it need?

A *Test a corner of the paper first to make sure that the colour will not bleed and that the pattern will not show through the paint colour. Make sure that the wallpaper is firmly stuck down and coat with a layer of thinned solvent-based paint before redecorating.*

Q How should I prepare new plasterboard for decorating?

A *Prime with plasterboard primer-sealer or with thinned latex paint and use size (a layer of wallpaper paste) on the walls. This makes it much easier to hang wallpaper and to strip it next time you decorate.*

Painting

Paint is a favorite with do it yourself decorators — and no wonder. It's relatively cheap, quick and easy to use, and though you need to take more care when preparing a surface for painting than you do for papering, the application itself is simple thanks to developments like one-coat wall paint, non-drip paint and latex paint, which make for easy application and cleanup. Paints like these are ideal for beginners — you can achieve excellent results without special skills. You may, however, want to use some of the other finishes on the market. The pages which follow may help you to understand how they perform and what effects they create.

Creating a mood with color — buttermilk walls and ceiling are cool and calm (below), whilst glowing honey tones provide a warm welcome (right).

Types of Paint

There are two main categories: latex paints, which are water-based, and solvent-based paints. You'll also find the latter called oil-based paints – a traditional if not always accurate description.

Latex paints

Modern latex paint offers a finish that is both easy to clean and resistant to wear. It is probably the most popular paint because of its wide selection of colours and ease of use. It will wash out of brushes – and clothes – when wet but is almost impossible to shift when dry, so take care not to spatter upholstery when you decorate.

Flat finish latex has a velvety, non-reflective quality, so it's a good choice for uneven walls. It can be wiped clean, but don't rub too hard, or too often, or it will become shiny or come off.

Semigloss latex enamel is shinier and more resistant to steam. It's recommended for kitchens and bathrooms though it's not as hardwearing as a solvent-based paint. It is also suitable for woodwork.

Latex paint is the one finish that can safely be used on new plaster, as it is porous and allows the moisture in the wall to evaporate. You can use latex over a sound, previously painted surface (with the exceptions of distemper and whitewash) but it's advisable to apply an initial 'fog' or 'mist' coat of emulsion thinned with water on new plaster or plasterboard to improve coverage. Your best bet is to use a primer coat first, however. Latex paints are quick-drying (allow two to four hours between coats), usually liquid in form and packaged in tin cans. One of the happiest developments for the do-it-yourself painter is latex paint that is guaranteed to cover in a single coat.

While such claims must be taken with a grain of salt, and more than one coat may be necessary if you are painting a light colour over a dark one, the fact remains that such paints save time and effort and are well worth their higher prices. One drawback, however, is the fact that they are not always available in a full range of colours.

Distemper is also a water-based paint, but don't expect to find it at a paint or art supply store. It has fallen from favour not only because it crumbles and it isn't moisture-resistant, but chiefly because it has to be completely removed before you can paint over it with anything else – even more distemper. On the plus side, it has an attractive chalky effect that is softer than that produced by modern latex paints. Interested? Then follow the recipe on pages 142-43 in the Special Finishes section to make and colour your own distemper.

Solvent- or oil-based paints

These paints are more durable and generally have a higher shine than latex. They should be thinned, and usually cleaned, with paint thinner.

Gloss enamel is the most familiar solvent-based paint but it's not really suitable for walls unless you want a wet-look finish! There are subtler ways of obtaining colour plus shine, as shown below. Gloss is usually reserved for wood and metalwork, where it provides a hard-wearing finish, though it is liable to chip if applied too thickly. Some gloss paints are only suitable for interior use; others are recommended for exteriors too, so check before you buy if you want a dual-purpose paint. Using gloss paint is often laborious, as two coats are usually

Paint should be chosen with care if it is to "go the distance". Here flat latex is used for wipe-clean walls – an essential quality in a hard-working kitchen – and furniture is protected by tough gloss.

required, and you need to be adept to avoid runs and brush marks. If you are painting over a prepainted surface, you should also bear in mind the fact that solvent-based paints should never be used over latex paints, or they will never dry completely. Consult your paint supplier before settling on an undercoat for your walls. Always work in a cool, well-ventilated room and shut the door when you finish so that the rest of the house is unaffected. Deck paint is rugged enamel-type paint suitable for interior floors and steps and other areas subject to a good deal of abuse. Varnish-based paints – the type most widely used – dry to a high-gloss finish.

Flat alkyd paint is another solvent-based paint. It has a fine finish and is somewhat more durable than flat latex paint. If this is what you require, you may be able to overlook the fact that it marks easily and is difficult to clean! To improve matters, finish with three coats of clear gloss varnish, a treatment that can also be used over ordinary latex paint to achieve sheen with a rich depth of colour.

Varnish can be used on walls as well as on woodwork. The most popular type is polyurethane varnish, which is available in flat, semigloss or gloss finish. Use it to protect delicate paints such as flat latex and undercoat and to seal decorative paint finishes to prolong their life and to postpone the fading of colour. Varnish can also be used to seal wood.

Suitability

Paint	Interior walls	Ceiling	Woodwork	Metalwork
flat latex	Yes	Yes	No	No
semigloss latex emulsion	Yes	Yes	Yes	No
distemper	Yes	Yes	No	No
alkyd gloss	Not recommended		Yes	Yes
alkyd semigloss	Yes	Yes	Yes	Yes

Coverage and Drying Times

Coverage will vary with the brand and the absorbency of the surface.
Times are approximate and depend on moderate, dry conditions.

Type of paint	Area covered per quart	Touch dry (in hours)	Recoatable (in hours)
flat latex	14-16sq yd	2	4
semigloss latex	15-18sq yd	2	4
alkyd gloss	20sq yd	12	16
non-drip gloss	16-19sq yd	1-3	5-6*
alkyd semigloss	13sq yd	12	16
alkyd flat	18sq yd	6	12
polyurethane varnish	19-20sq yd	3	16-24

* normally only one coat required

Equipment

Painting walls is fun because it's so fast. Brushes, rollers and pads are all designed to cover large areas quickly, but try them for size before you buy to see which suits you best. Don't choose the largest roller you can find to speed up the work unless you have strong wrists! Remember that you'll be using the same equipment to paint ceilings and that holding your arms above your head for any length of time is tiring.

Brushes are the pro's choice in most cases. Test them by running the bristles over your hand and discard any which shed hair copiously. Natural hog's hair brushes are the most expensive and absorb more paint than those with nylon bristles, but good quality nylon brushes are hard-wearing and easy to clean. Look for bristles with a tapered edge which allows you to 'lay off' or smooth the surface effectively. For painting large areas you'll need a 4 inch wall brush. Avoid the cheap sort which are best suited to pasting wallpaper, also the very wide 8 inch and wider brushes which are heavy to use. You'll also need a tapered cutting-in brush for painting the margins of walls where large brushes and rollers can't reach or won't cover accurately. Perfectionists will require a long-handled, angled crevice brush to reach behind pipes and similar obstructions.

Who should use a brush? Brushing is slow but sure. A wall brush will produce a fine finish without any hint of the 'orange peel' texture a roller may leave but in inexperienced hands the result may be flawed by brush marks. Beginners may find it difficult to create an even finish and should do better with a roller or paint pad. Everyone will need a cutting-in tool (brush or pad) to avoid a build-up of paint at the corners and to prevent smudges.

Rollers are the most popular choice for ceilings and walls. They are available in various widths (normally 8–12 inches) but although a wide roller will cover the wall more quickly, it can be heavy and unwieldy to use. Most rollers have a single frame like the ones shown here, but double frame rollers, where the sleeve is attached to the handle at both sides, are also available. The advantages are that you can apply a steady pressure and they are easier to use with an extension handle when painting high up, but they are more expensive than the single frame type and won't get as close to the corners. More important is to choose the right sleeve for the paint you're applying. And be sure to use separate rolls for latex and alkyd paints.

. . . foam is cheap enough to throw away after use, but its lack of absorbency may cause the paint to splash.

. . . lambswool, sheepskin or the synthetic equivalent are good, all-rounders suitable for use with the majority of paints. Choose a short pile for use on smooth surfaces, a long pile for reaching into textured ones. Do not use lambswool for enamel paint, however, which causes the wool to mat.

. . . mohair is most expensive but its fine pile is particularly suitable for applying shiny finishes.

Many rollers are sold complete with a tray, which is ridged for wiping away excess paint. You will also find small angled rollers for delving behind radiators and, like crevice brushes, they are also useful for painting behind pipes.

Who should use a roller? Anyone who wants to cover a surface fast and efficiently will find a roller ideal. The most common problems are spatter and stippling, both usually caused by overloading the roller though the quality of sleeve and paint may contribute. Cheap paint and cheap foam rollers may spray. Long pile rollers may cause cratering; again, the problem is particularly acute with semigloss latex.

Paint pads are lighter than rollers and are made in a range of sizes, from the tiny 1 × 2 inch pad for cutting-in to the large 4 × 8 inch type which is best for painting walls. They consist of fibre, or foamed urethane attached to a handle. Also available are disposable brush pads. These are available in widths up to 3 inches and eliminate brush cleanup. Paint pads give a smooth finish without spatter and are sometimes supplied with a tray.

Who should use a paint pad? Paint pads are perfect for beginners as they don't spray or leave brush marks. Use them on flat surfaces (a brush or long-pile roller works better on textures).

You will also need:

● a special opener for paint cans. Try not to use a screwdriver as it distorts the lid and makes it impossible to close properly. Instead, use the 'key' type tool sold at paint stores, a strong spoon or a tough round-bladed knife.

● a stick for stirring liquid paint. (Stirring non-drip paint makes it run!)

● a paint bucket if using a wall brush. Decanting paint into the bucket prevents solvent-based paints from forming a skin in the can during use, and a bucket is easier to manage than a large can. Add an S hook so that you can hang it up when necessary.

● a lint-free clean rag, moistened with paint thinner forms a home-made 'tack rag' to pick hairs off a freshly-painted wall and to erase mistakes when using solvent-based paint. Keep a similar cloth, dampened in water and dishwashing detergent, for wiping away splashes of latex paint.

● cleaning equipment. Lay this out before you start because the last thing you will want to do at the end of the day is to rummage around looking for jam jars, paint thinner and other brush cleaning solutions.

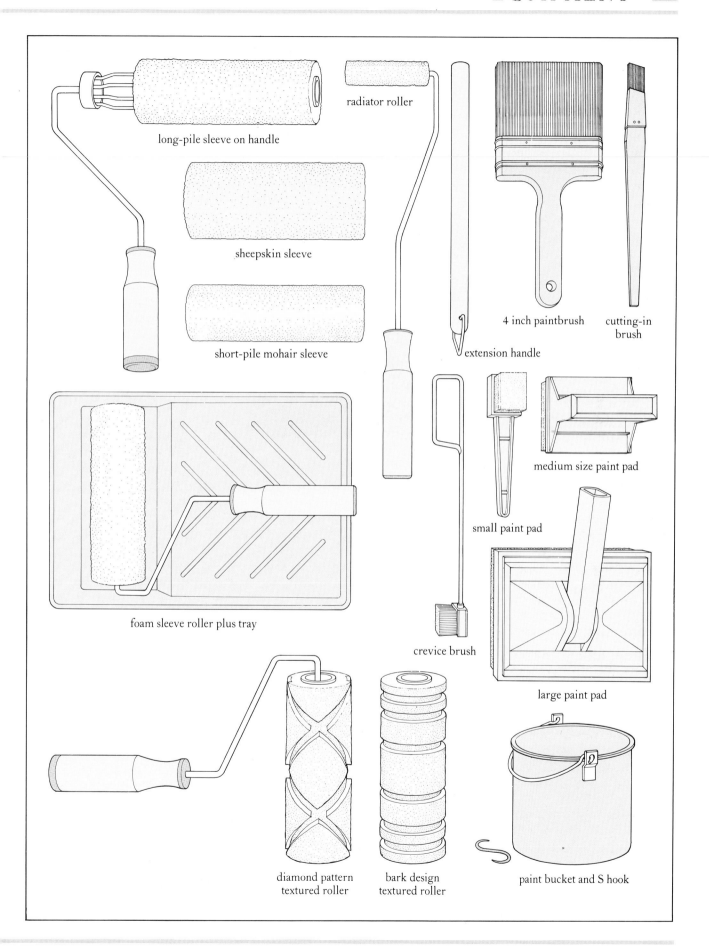

long-pile sleeve on handle

radiator roller

4 inch paintbrush

cutting-in brush

sheepskin sleeve

short-pile mohair sleeve

extension handle

medium size paint pad

small paint pad

foam sleeve roller plus tray

crevice brush

large paint pad

diamond pattern textured roller

bark design textured roller

paint bucket and S hook

Q I want a durable paint to use in the hall — something that I can wash down to clean off scuff marks and finger prints.
A *Pick a solvent-based paint with a mid-sheen finish to resist hard wear. (Semigloss latex enamel is also an option but remember that it is not as tough).*

Q What's happened to my radiator? I painted it to match the walls but now it's peeling and looks woolly.
A *You've used flat latex paint instead of a semigloss latex enamel or solvent-based paint. Next time you redecorate, use a gloss or semigloss paint if you want the radiator to blend with the background. For a tougher finish choose heat-resisting radiator enamel.*

Q Is there any substitute for solvent-based paints? I have asthma and find them unpleasant to use.
A *You can paint walls and woodwork with flat or semigloss latex paint. If you want to try treatments such as sponging or ragging, experiment with semigloss latex enamel.*

Q Which is the best paint to use in the kitchen?
A *Is your kitchen warm, dry and well-ventilated? Then you can choose from any of the finishes on the market. But if the windows steam up or the walls seem moist, you need a paint that will resist condensation. Semigloss latex enamel is a better choice than flat paints, but a solvent-based finish will resist dampness best.*

Equipment Care

Most latex paints can be washed out of equipment with dishwashing liquid and cool water, provided this is done as soon as the work is over. (Rinse first with cold water to remove the excess.) Some solvent-based paints respond to this treatment too, but always be guided by the instructions on the can. In most cases, you should clean tools used with solvent-based paints in paint thinner, turpentine or a commercial paint cleanser before washing in detergent solution and rinsing in cold water. Leave to dry and store flat. An ordinary jam jar is adequate for soaking brushes, but strictly speaking the brushes should be suspended in the liquid with a piece of string passed through a hole in the handle and tied to a pencil or stick balanced on top of the jar.

You can also invest in a gadget for cleaning brushes which clasps the handles in a detachable lid (see page 24). Don't leave brushes to soak

A flawless finish is only achieved by careful preparation and by thinking a scheme through thoroughly. This restful sitting room is completed with well-chosen accessories which pick up the hues of walls and woodwork.

indefinitely or the bristles will weaken and eventually go hard.

Clean rollers by removing the sleeve where possible. Don't forget to clean the handle to prevent a build-up of paint. The tray will also need to be washed or cleaned with paint thinner if you have been using solvent-based paint: use it to soak the roller in if necessary.

Paint pads may be difficult to clean because paint soaks into the rim, so are best reserved for latex paints which will wash out with detergent and water.

Naturally you won't want to go through the full routine when you stop for a break, so have a roll of plastic wrap handy to wrap round equipment to keep it moist.

Sequence of Painting

Always start at the highest point, so begin by painting the ceiling (pp. 52-55). Then tackle walls, window frames, picture rail (if any), doors and baseboard in order. Work away from the light from the top downwards, starting in the right hand corner unless you are left-handed. Before you tackle the main wall surface, use a small brush or pad to paint corners, above baseboards and below picture rails, around windows and doors, and any other awkward areas which are inaccessible with a large brush, roller or pad. This technique is called 'cutting in' and will help you avoid a visible joining line when you come to paint the rest of the wall.

Painting Techniques

Different types of paint require different methods of application. Follow the step-by-step techniques here and on page 24 for success.

Paint walls in horizontal bands, working downwards and away from the light as shown in the diagram below.

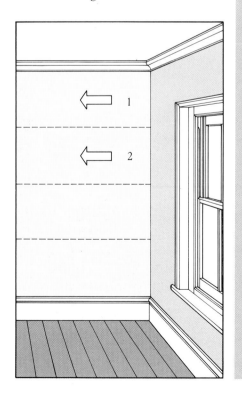

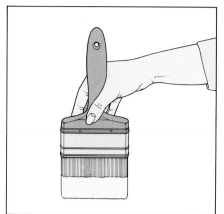

1

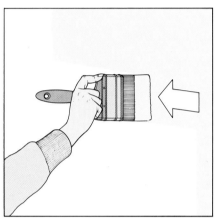

2

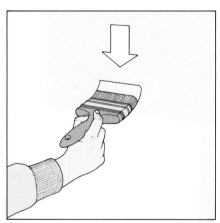

3

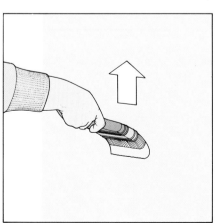

4

Using a wall brush

Hold a wall brush close to the 'stock' (the part bonded to the bristles) and dip it into the paint until the bristles are half covered. Squeeze the excess against the side of the paint bucket or can, not against the rim where it may dry in lumps which fall into the paint.

Latex Paint

Start at the top of the wall and work away from the light in horizontal bands about 30 inches wide.

Follow the sideways brushing action by 'laying off' with feather-light strokes to remove brush-marks. Use light downward strokes on the top half of the wall.

When you are painting the lower half, lay off in the same way, but this time use gentle upward strokes to prevent drips and runs.

Solvent-based paint

Solvent-based paint is more difficult to manipulate than latex so tackle a smaller area at a time. Work from the top of the wall downward in squares and begin with downward strokes.

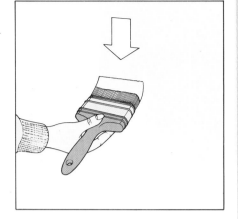

Without reloading the brush, spread the paint across in a horizontal direction to cover the square completely.

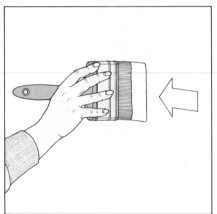

Finish by 'laying off' with light upward strokes. When you have finished the first row of squares, begin again from the top of the wall, overlapping slightly so that the edges merge.

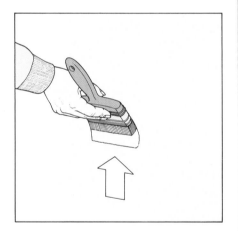

Cleaning brushes

Brushes used with most solvent-based paints should be cleaned with paint thinner (check with the directions); latex paint usually washes out with detergent and water. If you need to soak the brushes suspend them in the solution or use a special gadget, to protect the bristles.

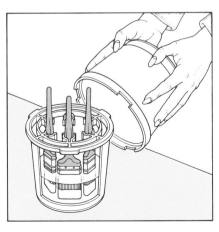

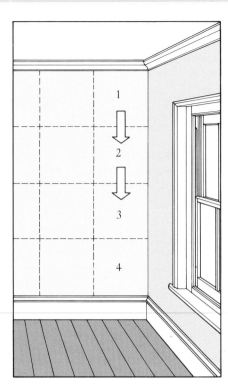

Work from the top down in squares. Start with downward strokes and then, without reloading the brush, spread the paint across to bridge the gaps. Finish by 'laying off' with light upward strokes. Tackle the next square below until the column is complete as illustrated above.

Making an entrance – a sunny hallway always gives a good first impression.

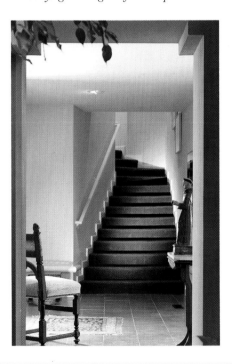

Roller and pad techniques

With a roller . . . pour sufficient paint into the tray to fill the lower third – no more or the ridges intended to remove excess paint from the sleeve cannot function. Dip the roller into the paint and slide it backwards and forwards in the shallow end of the tray to remove the surplus.

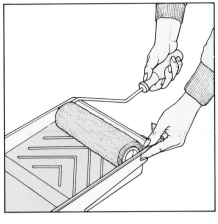

Angle the roller to cover the wall in a criss-cross pattern to obliterate directional marks.

With a paint pad . . . dip the large pad into the tray or can, squeezing to remove the excess and work in regular bands, moving up and down the wall.

Use a small paint pad to outline the edges of walls, windows and doors and to paint other awkward areas.

First Aid

Faults in painting are usually due to impatience – lack of care during preparation or overloading the brush or roller!

Blisters . . . are caused by painting on a damp surface or soft existing paint. Give the paint ten days to harden, then sand down, clean, and cure the damp or remove the defective paint before repainting.

Brushmarks . . . result from overloading the brush or using one which has hardened because it was not thoroughly cleaned. When the paint has dried completely, rub down and repaint using a new brush, taking care not to overload it.

Cratering . . . is caused by condensation forming on the surface before the paint is dry. Sand when dry and repaint, keeping the room warm and well-ventilated.

Crazing . . . comes from applying a top coat while the one beneath is still tacky. Allow to dry thoroughly then rub down and repaint.

Flaking . . . occurs if the surface beneath is powdery. Rub down when dry and treat the wall beneath by sanding, then coat with stabilising solution if necessary.

Runs and wrinkles . . . happen when you overload the brush. If there are only a few you may get away with puncturing the run, sanding down and touching in; otherwise sand down completely, clean and repaint.

Specks . . . are caused by dust and grit trapped in the drying paintwork. Allow to dry and sand down before repainting.

Variations in colour . . . occur when you buy paint from different batches or you stop work for the day without completing a wall. Assess how much paint you will require and buy it all at the same time. Always finish a section at a time whether you're painting a wall, window frame or baseboard so that seams are not noticeable.

Painted Textures

Think beyond a quick lick of latex paint or a trip to the local wallpaper shop! Instead of considering bare brick or plaster as a problem to be disguised, turn them to your advantage. Surfaces such as these present an ideal opportunity to introduce interesting textures into your room and lend themselves well to the type of imaginative treatment illustrated here.

Top left: the walls of this cosy dining room were colour washed before the plaster dried out properly to give a marvellous mottled effect.

Top centre: a garden inside the home – painted brick walls, colourful plants and garden chairs give this conservatory an authentic outdoor feel.

Top right: if your brickwork is rather unsightly, the walls can be rendered in either a smooth or subtly textured finish, then painted over.

Bottom left: a perfect backdrop for antique furniture, whitewashed stone walls are washed with a transparent brownish glaze for a mellow look.

Bottom centre: paint contrasting colours above and below the dado rail for added interest.

Bottom right: this bathroom has been treated in classic Mediterranean fashion, its cool stone walls whitewashed to reflect every ray of sunshine.

Wall-coverings

Wallpaper dresses up plain walls. You can add pattern, texture, or both, in a variety of materials which range from hard-wearing vinyl to delicate grasscloth and silk. Plastic now rivals paper in popularity, and there are an increasing number of ranges designed to be simple to hang and easy to care for. We give you an explanation of the qualities of the various types of paper and the ease with which they can be hung, plus details of how to achieve a really professional finish.

Speckled wallpaper makes a plain but interesting surface against which to display favourite pictures and teams perfectly with co-ordinating border and furnishings (right), whilst marbled wallpaper is an excellent solution to the problem of how to lend texture to large areas such as walls (below).

Wallcoverings give you the opportunity to add pattern and texture as well as colour to your walls. They can be more than merely decorative — a thick relief wallcovering will help disguise uneven plaster while one made from vinyl will withstand repeated washing.

When choosing a design, bear in mind that you'll often be covering large surfaces in the room with pattern, so it's worth taking special care to assess its impact. Note that while big, boldly coloured patterns will appear to reduce space, small on a pale ground will seem to increase it because they give the effect of 'looking through' the design. Avoid stripes unless you have a cornice, coving or picture rail and regular walls, and keep to small random designs if the plaster is irregular or the walls are out of true. Pick an inexpensive medium weight wallpaper for your first attempt at wallpapering.

The asterisks * used in the following information denote ease of use for the amateur. The more stars, the easier the product is to apply.

Types of Wallcovering

Lining papers

These provide a smooth ground for wallcoverings or paint. Hang them horizontally beneath wallcoverings so that the seams don't overlap. Hang them vertically if you're going to paint on top. They come in several weights: light – for covering with paint; medium – which is recommended for most wallpapers; heavy – for supporting relief or vinyl wallcoverings.
Rating: **

Cotton-backed lining paper helps to stabilise flexible surfaces such as wallboard or tongue and groove boarding.
Rating: *

Expanded polystyrene will insulate a wall and provide a base for conventional wallpaper on uneven walls.
Rating: *

Wallcovering for painting

Embossed wallpaper has a textured design created by pressure from a metal roller. The uncoloured off-white type is intended as a base for paint.
Rating: **

High relief wallcoverings have a more pronounced design. They may be made from wood pulp, like embossed papers, plus cotton and clay, or from blown vinyl where specific areas are coated with chemical and then baked so that the design rises.
Rating: **

Only vinyl relief wallcoverings are inherently washable; with other relief wallcoverings, the paint protects the paper while the paper disguises defects in the wall. Many relief wallcoverings must be finished with latex paint – choose a semigloss paint to highlight the effect.

Printed wallcoverings

Borders can be used to follow door frames, baseboards, dados and picture rails. They are often designed to co-ordinate with wallpapers and upholstery fabrics and are made from standard wallpaper. Some wallpapers are dual-purpose: they can be used as a striped pattern or cut into strips to create a border.
Rating: **

Friezes are generally deeper than borders and are hung at picture rail level. They may co-ordinate with borders, wallpapers and soft furnishings and are made from standard wallpaper.
Rating: **

Hand-printed wallpapers have designs created by blocks or screens instead of machines. Because it's necessary to use a separate block or screen for every colour, multi-coloured designs are very expensive. Hand-printing is a craft, so expect some variation in colour and design

to occur. The papers are often untrimmed so you will need a professional wallpaper cutting wheel if you intend to hang them yourself. These papers are obviously best installed by professionals or the dealers from whom you buy them.
Rating: not recommended for amateurs

Metallic foils are plastic-based. They should be used with care because they emphasize irregularities in the wall, crease easily and conduct electricity, so they should never be tucked behind a light switch or socket.
Rating: *

Polyethylene foam is light and flat. There is no backing paper so it is easy to strip, and as the wall is pasted rather than the wallcovering it is easy to hang and ideal for tricky areas like ceilings if you take care not to stretch it.
Rating: **

Ready-pasted wallcoverings are coated with adhesive during manufacture. This is activated by placing the wallcovering in a trough of water before hanging. Keep a tube of latex adhesive on hand to touch in the corners where the adhesive may be thinly applied, or keep a small amount of ordinary paste and a brush handy to repaste any edges which dry out while the paper is being hung.
Rating: ***

Standard wallpapers are either pulp, where the pattern is printed directly on to the paper surface, or made from paper coated with a ground colour before the pattern is applied. Weights vary, so choose a medium weight paper rather than a flimsy one which is liable to tear when wet with paste.
Rating: medium weight ***

Vinyl wallcoverings have a pattern printed directly on to plastic, making the surface so durable that some

can be scrubbed. All vinyls are dry-strippable because they have a paper backing. Tile patterns are often seen on blown vinyl, made in the same way as vinyl relief wall-coverings to create a substitute for wall tiles that's almost as thick as flooring. Some vinyls are pre-pasted, otherwise hang with a fungicidal paste. Where overlapping is unavoidable a special adhesive must be used.
Rating: conventional vinyl ***, blown vinyl **

Washable and spongeable wallpapers are finished with a film of clear plastic to protect the design. They are sometimes dry-strippable, leaving a plain paper backing on the wall as a surface for redecoration, and may be pre-pasted.
Rating: ***

Textured wallcoverings
Coloured embossed papers are made in exactly the same way as those intended for painting.
Rating: **

Cork is expensive. It is made from slivers of cork mounted on a paper backing, normally coloured green, black or red. Use a special adhesive and avoid marking the surface.
Rating: *

Felt is normally paper-backed. It is available in a range of colours but deep shades are liable to fade.
Rating: *

Flocks can be made from paper plus silk, cotton or wool, or from vinyl with nylon fibres. In each case the background has a velvety texture and the pattern is formed by applying adhesive to selected areas to trap the fibres. Vinyl/nylon flock is very hard-wearing but care should be taken when hanging flock that's made from natural fibres as excess paste may stain the surface.
Rating: *

Grasscloth is held in place by cotton on a paper backing. It is delicate, expensive and difficult to clean. Special adhesive is required.
Rating: not recommended for amateurs

Burlap is sold both unbacked and paper-backed. As with felt, deep colours may fade. The paper-backed type is far easier to hang and is recommended for use by amateurs.
Rating: paper-backed **

Silk is one of the most popular fabrics used as a wallcovering. (A synthetic equivalent is also available.) It is luxurious but very expensive and difficult to clean.
Rating: not recommended for amateurs

Pattern Matching

Free-match wallcoverings have a random design that doesn't need to be matched. Off-set match or drop patterns produce a diagonal effect. Adjoining lengths of wallcovering must be moved up or down to line up the design correctly. Set or straight match wallcoverings have patterns which line up horizontally.

Look for information on wallcoverings at the back of the roll or pattern book.

Imported wallpapers may summarize this information in symbols.

Pattern repeats measure the distance from the top of the design to where it starts again. The larger the size of the repeat, the more wastage there's likely to be. Allow for repeats when estimating quantity.

Ask the Professionals

Q The plaster in my dining room, painted at present, is patchy and irregular. I'd like to paper it but I don't know what to choose.
A *If you want to use a patterned wallpaper, you should line (and possibly cross-line) the walls first with medium-weight lining paper. Choose a medium-weight wallpaper with a random design which will help to disguise imperfections and remember to allow the paste time to soak in so that the paper doesn't stretch and bubble on the walls. Opt for a discreet or abstract pattern like basket-weave if your room is small; if it's large you can afford to choose a more elaborate design.*

Q Which is the best wallcovering to use on plasterboard walls?
A *Because plasterboard is so absorbent, prepare the walls first with size (made from dilute wallpaper paste) – this makes it easier to slip the wallpaper into place. Don't use an embossed wallpaper as a base for paint; instead choose a relief vinyl with a paper backing which remains on the wall when the vinyl is removed. All vinyls, and dry-strippable washable wallpapers, have a similar backing which makes redecoration easier; polyethylene foam is also simple to strip. There's no reason why you should not use standard wallpaper, but be prepared for problems when you remove it.*

Roll size

Most rolls of wallcovering measure 27 inches wide. (Imported sizes may differ.) Textile wallcoverings are often sold by the yard.

Once you know the roll-size of the wallcovering you've chosen you can use a calculator to work out how much you'll require. For ready reference, the guide below shows the number of standard single rolls you will probably need.

Adhesives

Cellulose powder added to water forms a general-purpose adhesive suitable for most standard wallpapers. The exceptions are high relief designs and textile wallcoverings like burlap and grasscloth which require a stronger paste. (Always follow the wallcovering manufacturer's recommendations when buying adhesive.)

Adhesives with fungicide must be used with any plastic wallcovering – wallpaper, vinyl, or polyethylene foam, or if you are papering over any plastic-coated product, whether it's washable wallpaper or laminated wall board. Because plastic does not allow moisture to evaporate, there's always a chance that mould may form on the wall unless a fungicide is used. These adhesives are poisonous, so keep them away from children.

Ready-mixed adhesive is also available. It's generally designed for heavy wallcoverings.

Ready-pasted wallcoverings don't require paste. This is applied to the backing during manufacture and is activated by soaking in water.

Size is made from diluted powder adhesive. It's an excellent idea to brush a coat of size on to the wall before you paper as it leaves a smooth slightly slippery surface which helps when aligning adjoining lengths of paper. You'll find instructions for making size on the back of most packs of paste.

Imported Wallcovering Symbols Chart

~	spongeable
≈	washable
≋	super-washable
▤	scrubbable
☼	sufficient light fastness
☼	good light fastness
⌐	strippable
⌐	peelable (leaves backing)
⊌	ready-pasted
▐	paste the wall
→│∘	free match
→│←	straight match
→│	off-set match (half drop)
50cm/25	design repeat distance off-set
⧚	duplex (layered)
⧢	co-ordinated fabric available
↑	direction of hanging
↑↓	reverse alternate lengths

Imported Wallpapers: Calculating number of rolls required

Height of wall	Measurement around room in feet											
Feet	28	32	40	44	52	56	60	64	68	72	80	84
7-7½	4	4	5	6	7	7	8	8	9	9	10	10
7½-8	4	4	5	6	7	8	8	9	9	10	11	11
8-8½	4	5	6	7	8	8	9	9	10	11	12	12
8½-9	4	5	6	7	8	9	9	10	10	11	12	13
9½-10	5	6	7	7	9	9	10	10	11	12	13	14
10-10½	5	6	7	8	9	10	10	11	12	12	14	14
10½-11½	5	6	7	8	9	10	11	11	12	13	14	15

American Wallpapers: Calculating number of rolls required

Height of wall	Measurement around room in feet											
Feet	28	36	44	52	60	68	72	80	88	92	96
8	7	9	11	13	15	17	18	20	22	23	24
9	8	10	12	15	17	19	20	22	24	26	27
10	9	11	14	16	19	21	22	25	27	28	30
11	10	12	15	18	20	23	24	27	30	31	32
12	11	13	16	19	22	25	27	30	32	34	35
14	12	16	19	22	26	29	31	34	38	39	41

Equipment

You will need:
- a pasting brush. You can buy a special brush with synthetic bristles that's easy to clean (soak in water and dishwashing liquid after use), but an ordinary wall brush for painting walls will do.
- a smoothing or paperhanger's brush. You can compromise with a sponge but this is the best tool for smoothing down standard paper.
- a damp sponge to wipe paste from the surface of the wallcovering. Use it dry for smoothing embossed wallpaper which may flatten under pressure.
- a steel tape measure, for measuring lengths.
- a trimming knife, or small scissors, for cutting round light switches.
- a pencil, for marking levels, screw holes and vertical lines on the wall as a guide.
- a pair of shears or long scissors for cutting lengths.
- a plumb bob and line. It's important to make sure that the first length you hang is straight as it sets the rule for each subsequent one.
- a seam roller to press down the seams. Never use a seam roller on textured wallpaper or it may crush the design and make the seams more noticeable.
- a pasting table. It's worth buying because it's the right shape for papering, folds for storage and costs very little. Most pasting tables measure 3 × 6 feet.
- a plastic bucket for wallpaper paste. Tying a piece of taut string to each end of the handle is a decorator's trick which gives you somewhere to rest the brush and to wipe away excess paste. A plastic trash bag inside the bucket overcomes the problem of disposing of paste.
- a trough for soaking ready-pasted wallcoverings, if required (usually supplied with the wallcovering).
- a stepladder.

smoothing or paperhanger's brush

pasting brush

sponge

trimming knife

plumb bob and line

steel tape measure   pencil   shears   seam roller

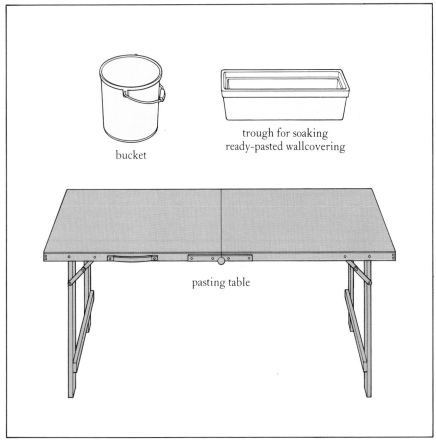

bucket

trough for soaking ready-pasted wallcovering

pasting table

Wall-coverings

Whichever covering you finally opt for, choose with care as walls present the largest surface area in a room and play a large part in determining its mood.

Top, far left: wood panelling stands in all its original splendour.

Top left: burlap-covered walls tone well with a cream and brown scheme.

Top right: striped wallpaper in seaside colours is jolly yet formal enough for entertaining guests.

Bottom, far left: cork tiles not only look and feel warm, they also constitute an insulating layer.

Bottom, centre left: plain latex looks best on a subtly textured paper.

Bottom left: tongue-and-groove pine paneling can hide poor-quality plasterwork and is highly practical.

Bottom right: this Regency drawing room and its genuine period furniture are set off by simple trellis paper.

Papering: where to start

Although it's wise to work away from the light – such as a window – so that the seams are less noticeable, this isn't the main consideration. The most important point is to avoid joining lengths in a prominent place, like the centre of a chimney breast, especially if the design is pronounced. (Sometimes, however, you may find that you have to join two pieces of paper at the centre of a chimney breast to ensure that any large motif is centred.)

Here are some guidelines which may help.

Do you have:

. . . a simple rectangular room without alcoves and with only one window? (This is the easiest set-up for beginners to deal with.) Start at the corner nearest the door and work round until you come back to base.

. . . a room with a chimney breast? Position the first length in the centre of the chimney breast. Treat each half of the room separately, working outwards from one side of the

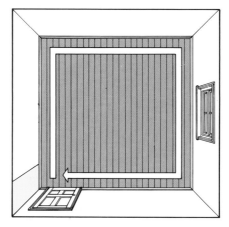
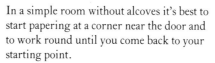
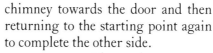

In a simple room without alcoves it's best to start papering at a corner near the door and to work round until you come back to your starting point.

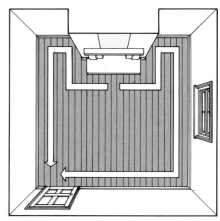

In a room with a chimney breast, centre the design at its centre and work outwards down the side walls until you reach the door.

chimney towards the door and then returning to the starting point again to complete the other side.

. . . a room with one large or two medium-size windows on one wall? Butt the first length of wallpaper against the right hand window and work your way round to the end of the adjacent wall. (This helps you, literally, to get the hang of it and to make any errors in the least conspicuous place.) Next paper the rest of the window wall and the left hand side wall. Finally, decorate the far wall.

Finding the vertical

Walls are rarely straight so you must mark a vertical line as a guide before you begin papering if you want perfect results. For this you'll need a plumb bob and line, which is simply a weight on a piece of string. (If you're starting at the corner of the room, draw your guideline about 1 inch less than a roll's width from the corner because you'll need to turn a similar amount on to the adjoining wall.) Hold the line steady at ceiling level and make sure the 'bob' at the end of the line reaches the baseboard. Mark its position in three places with a pencil (if possible get someone to do this while you hold the line) and join them up, using a wooden slat or yardstick. Hang the first length of wallpaper to this line. Each time you reach a 'new' wall you have to mark a vertical line as a guide to hanging the first length on that wall.

To find the vertical, hold the plumb bob and line steady and mark its position in three places (far left). Join them up with a straight pencil line to establish the true vertical (left).

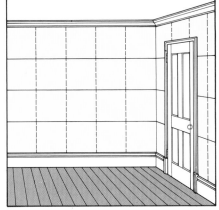

Line walls horizontally (top). If the condition is poor, cross-line, first vertically then horizontally (above).

Lining walls

Lining the walls improves the end result if you're using a thin wallpaper, or if your walls are irregular. Lining paper is hung horizontally so that the seams won't coincide with those of the top layer. (Try not to join lengths as this will make the lining conspicuous.) If your walls are in poor condition consider cross-lining them with two layers of paper; the first layer hung vertically, the second horizontally.

To line walls horizontally, work from the top downwards. Mark a straight edge 1 inch less than a roll's width from the ceiling to allow for the overlap and allow about ¾ inch at each end for turning the corners. Butt-join succeeding lengths and trim the excess at the baseboard (see below). It's best to tackle this task with a partner.

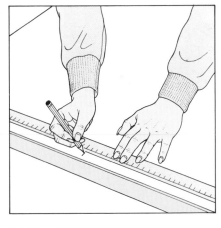

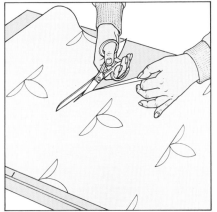

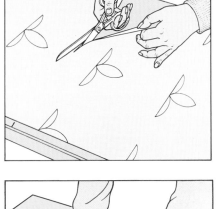

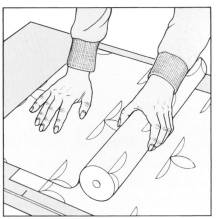

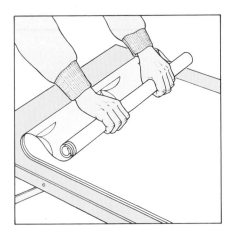

Cutting

Cutting must be done with care. Professionals usually cut all the drops before they begin so they only have to measure once but you may find it easier to complete one wall at a time if you are decorating a large room.

Mark the edge of your pasting table in 1 foot sections for ready reference.

Measure the wall and add a 6 inch trimming allowance. Lay the wallpaper face up on the pasting table and cut your first length.

Using this as a guide, cut the remaining drops. Cut equal lengths of random designs but match up patterns carefully before you reach for the scissors. Remember to allow 6 inches for trimming at ceiling and baseboard with each length.

Roll the lengths of paper against the curl to flatten them. Turn the pile of cut lengths over so that the surface for pasting is uppermost. (This will be the first drop that you cut.) You are now ready to paste.

Ask the Professionals

Q Which is the easiest wall-covering for a novice to apply? I'd like to try my hand at papering but I don't want it to be a waste of time and money.

A *If you want to acquire traditional skills, consider using a standard medium-weight wallpaper. Ready-pasted vinyl wallcovering is also simple to hang; you don't have to worry about adhesive as this is activated when you soak it in water in the trough provided. However, it is worth having a little ready-mixed adhesive to hand to stick down the corners securely. Whatever you choose, make sure that it's a free-match design so that you don't have to align the pattern. Matching the pattern can be tedious and difficult and is best left to more experienced wallpaper hangers.*

Q Should I try to hang textile wallcovering myself?

A *Not unless you are experienced at paper hanging. The problem is not that paper-backed textile wallcoverings are especially difficult to hang, but that they are so expensive that any mistake may prove a disaster. If you want to try, choose an inexpensive type like paper-backed burlap or a very light one, such as cork. Make sure you use the right adhesive and take care not to smear the surface of the wallcovering. Don't attempt to hang grasscloth or silk unless you are particularly adept.*

1

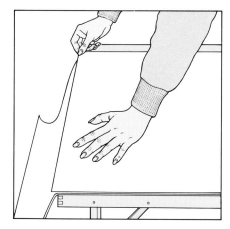

2

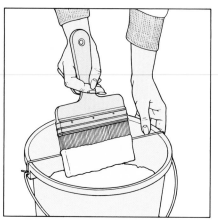

3

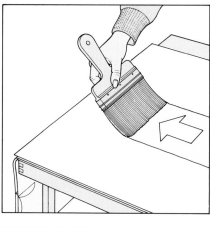

4

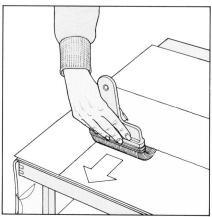

Pasting

Mix the paste according to the manufacturer's instructions. (Use a thinner mixture with a thin paper, thicker paste for a heavy one.)

Place the lengths so that they overlap the table slightly at the end. Pull the top one towards you and push the rest so that they overhang to prevent paste from smudging the surface of the wallpaper.

Dip the brush in the paste bucket and wipe the excess on the string.

Make sure that you don't have too much paste on the brush. Now paste a strip along the centre of the paper, starting at the short edge.

Brush the paste away from you and then to the front. Carefully fold the pasted ends over to the middle (see top right) and repeat the process on the rest.

Fold this over and leave on one side to soak. Leave medium weight paper for five minutes (ten for heavy paper) before hanging. Thin papers and vinyls can be hung immediately. Don't rush — if a paper is not fully stretched it will expand and crease on the wall.

Ready-pasted wallcoverings

These should be soaked in the special water trough provided. Roll each length so that the pattern is inside and put it in the trough for the required time – usually around a minute. Then lift it out by the top corners and smooth into place with a sponge. Run over the seams with a seam roller and keep a small amount of paste and a brush handy to use if the wallcovering shows a tendency to lift at the edges.

Potential Problems

Gaps occur when the paper dries out and shrinks. They are sometimes caused by handling the paper too much and excessive brushing out, which stretches it to a deceptive extent. Since gaps will occur only after the paper has been in place for some time you will probably have to strip it off and repaper.

Lumps and bumps may show through from the wall beneath. There's little you can do but strip off the wallcovering and start again by lining the walls. An embossed or high-relief wallcovering may overcome the problem.

Bubbles and wrinkles may be due to lack of pasting, not allowing sufficient soaking time or not brushing the paper carefully on to the wall, thus trapping air underneath the paper. You can overcome the odd bubble by cutting a cross through it with a sharp knife, pasting the four flaps of paper and then brushing it back into place. If there are a lot of bubbles, hang new paper after stripping off the defective length.

Peeling Damp is a common cause of peeling and needs to be dealt with before you decorate. If this isn't the problem, try sizing the wall with diluted wallpaper paste.

Tears need not be a disaster. You can usually stick them back so that they're inconspicuous, though major tears may lead you to discard the length and start afresh.

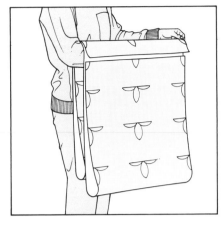

1

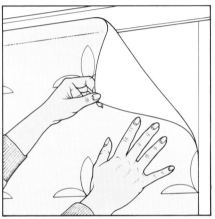

2

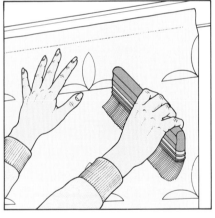

3

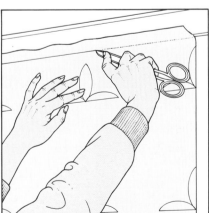

4

Hanging

Hanging the wallcovering should now be easy.

Pick up the folded length and drape it over your arm. Note which is the top. To avoid errors, you should write TOP in pencil on the relevant edge before pasting a length.

Open out the top half of the length; place the edge of the paper against your vertical line, allowing 3 inches for trimming at the top and 1 inch along the adjacent wall if you're turning a corner.

Brush down with the smoothing brush, then move out to the edges and up, to remove bubbles and creases. When the top half of the paper is in position, open out the bottom half and lower it gently – don't let it drop down or the paper will stretch unevenly.

Smooth out the lower half with the brush. Crease the paper at the ceiling with scissors or a pencil to give you a guide for cutting wallpaper.
(Continued on page 40)

Hanging (continued)

Cut away the waste following the crease line carefully with a sharp pair of scissors.

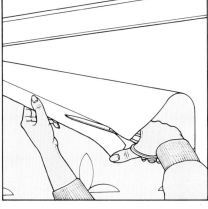

5

Smooth the top back into place with a brush so that it lies perfectly flat. Trim the base similarly flush with the baseboard.

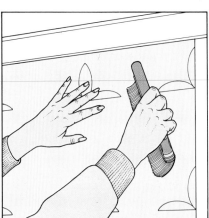

6

Line up the second length with the first, making sure that the patterns match. Push it tightly up to the first drop (the paper will shrink as it dries so there'll be a gap if you don't) to form a butt joint. After the paper has been in place for five minutes, press along the seam with a brush or seam roller unless you are hanging embossed or relief wallcoverings where you may crush the design.

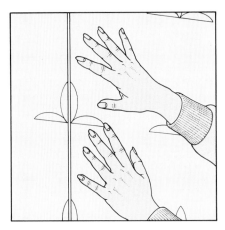

7

Papering round corners

Cut the last drop of wallpaper so that it overlaps the corner by about 1 inch. Now mark the vertical on the wall (you should do this every time you turn a corner when papering) and hang the first drop so that it covers the margin.

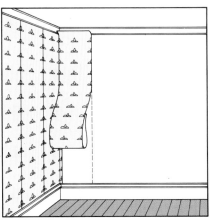

Coping with Obstacles

Papering techniques for tricky areas are basic but require care.

Corners

Don't try to paste a complete width of wallpaper round a corner – it will be crooked and creased. You will have to overlap lengths so you won't be able to match the pattern exactly but try to make seams as discreet as possible. For internal corners (see bottom right) measure from the edge of the last length to the corner. Measure at the top, bottom and the centre and add 1 inch to the largest measurement. Cut this amount from the next length. Paste into place taking 1 inch around the corner. Use the remaining piece on the adjacent wall, covering the overlap, but make sure it is hung to a true vertical on the 'new wall'. When using embossed wallpaper, 'feather' the edge of the overlap by tearing it and press down the remainder with a seam roller to remove bulk. For external corners follow the same procedure, positioning the turn where it will be least obvious, inside an alcove for example. Hang the next piece from your vertical guide line on the next wall so that it covers the margin. This avoids positioning seams on exposed edges where they will tear.

Window sills and projecting frames

One way to deal with window sills is to pull the paper over the projecting edge of the sill, cut round it, and then press the paper into place. You can use scraps to paper the wall above and below a flush window, but take care to match the pattern to the adjoining length. Scraps can also be used when papering a window recess; remember to avoid seams on the edge which will tear if knocked. Treat the edges like corners, overlapping the paper rather than butt-joining it.

Light switches

Light switches fall into two categories. Treat them in the same way to start with, draping the wallcovering over them and pressing down lightly to leave a mark on the underside.

To accommodate an old-fashioned projecting switch, pull the wallcovering up and cut four diagonal slits from the centre of the mark outwards.

Fit this round the light switch, cut off the excess and smooth into place.

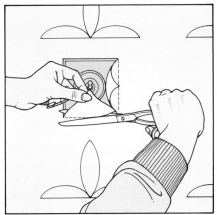

For flush switches, turn off the electricity first. Remove the cover and paste the wallcovering over the backplate. Cut away the square of paper, leaving a ¼ inch margin.

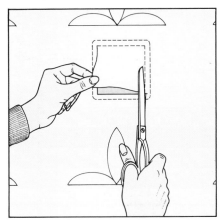

Replace the cover, tucking in the rim of paper for a neat finish.

DO NOT attempt this with metallic foil wallcoverings as they conduct electricity.

Stairwells

Stairwell walls are tricky because of the lengths involved and the problem of access. Make sure you set up a safe work station (see page 11) and get assistance if you can. Start at the point where you can paste the longest drop and work in the maximum number of complete widths. Use your plumb bob and line to mark the vertical, but this time run chalk along the string and pin it to the top of the wall. Snap it against the wall so that it leaves a straight line.

You'll have to cut and measure each length separately, and remember that you'll need to allow extra to fit the angled baseboard as you go downstairs (see below). Concertina long lengths of wallcovering, folding pasted edge to pasted edge, for easier carrying.

Remember to allow enough paper to take in the angled baseboard.

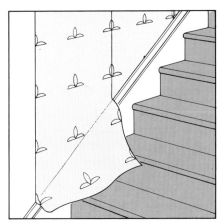

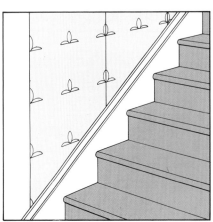

Tiling

Tiles are the most durable of all wallcoverings.
There is a great variety of tiles available, so it's
worth knowing about the different types and the
uses to which they're suited. Use them to form a
seal around baths, sinks and showers, in colours
which blend with fabric, flooring or wallcovering.
You'll find patterns to complement other
furnishings too — perfect for a completely co-
ordinated room scheme for kitchen,
bathroom or bedroom.

*As well as being immensely practical in kitchens and
bathrooms, tiles used with flair can look stylish, too.
Ceramic tiles are broken up visually with a thin line of
grout to echo the border on blind and mat (right). And in a
small kitchen, Victorian-style tiles on walls and floor make
an ideal, easy-to-clean surface.*

Ceramic tiles create a smart, hard-wearing surface behind the stove and around worktops, showers and baths. All ceramic tiles must be grouted; if you were to butt them against each other there would be no room for expansion and the tiles would buckle and crack. Grouting seals this gap and protects it from damp. (Remember that if you want the area to be completely water-proof, you'll need to use water-resistant adhesive and grout and allow a week for the tiles to dry out before you turn on the tap.) As one batch of tiles may vary slightly in colour from the next, it is a good idea to mix them beforehand. Tiles are available in four types and a number of sizes.

Universal tiles have four square edges with either two adjacent sides or all four sides having glazed edges. There's no difference between top and bottom (hence the name) and you'll need to use matchsticks or little plastic spacers between them to achieve an even grouting space. With bevelled-edged (angled) universal tiles, however, spacers are not needed.

Spacer tiles have a rim round the edge or small projections called lugs which automatically set the distance between tiles.

Mosaic tiles are tiny squares stuck on to a backing sheet which is fixed to the wall with adhesive. Individual tiles can be peeled off for tiling round fixtures so they can be useful for areas cluttered with pipes and other obstacles.

The most common tile sizes are 4¼ inches square, ¼ inch thick, and 6 inches square, ¼ inch thick. You'll also find rectangular tiles: 8 by 4 inches, ¼ inch thick, and 8 by 6 inches, ¼ inch thick, are two popular sizes. Mosaic tiles measure from ¾ inch square to 2 inches square and are supplied on sheets; popular sizes for these are approximately 12 inches square and 24 by 12 inches. Ceramic floor tiles are larger, thicker and less highly glazed than those designed for walls, though you can use them there if you wish. They may be suitable for worktops too, but don't try to use wall tiles for floors – they are slippery and will crack.

Mirror tiles often have self-adhesive pads on the back. Sizes are similar to those for ceramic tiles – 4 ¼ and 6 inches square – but you'll find large tiles 12 or 16 inches square as well – these reflect a less broken image. You'll need a glass cutter for cutting mirror tiles, but they don't require grouting.

Cork tiles insulate the wall and provide a pin-board surface. They are available sealed or unsealed for floor or wall use though dark brown insulating cork should only be used for walls. They need a special cork adhesive. The most popular size is 12 inches square.

First Steps

It's tempting to neglect preparation knowing that the tiles will camouflage the wall beneath, but unless the base is clean, sound and level the tiles won't adhere or you won't be able to hang them neatly. Here's how to prepare different surfaces.

Latex paint. Wash down the walls with diluted detergent and rinse.

Solvent-based paint. Remove any flaking paint and rub down the wall with coarse sandpaper so the adhesive will adhere. Wash down with detergent and rinse.

New plaster. Wait until the wall is completely dry, then apply a coat of sealer primer.

Plasterboard. Wipe down with paint thinner and coat with primer.

Wallpaper. Strip it off before you tile. *Don't* tile over it as the weight of the tiles will bring the whole lot down.

Wood. Make sure the surface is stable. Paint with wood primer.

Old tiles. You can tile on top of tiles satisfactorily (after all, they're doing

This imaginative yet practical use of toning ceramic tiles makes a bold visual statement.

Calculating the number of tiles

Area in square yards	Number of tiles — Size of tiles in inches			
	4¼ by 4¼	6 by 6	4 by 8	12 by 12
1	100	44	50	12
2	200	87	100	23
3	300	130	150	34
5	400	174	200	45
6	500	217	250	56
7	600	260	300	67
8	700	303	350	78
9	800	347	400	89
10	900	390	450	100
11	1000	433	500	111

it in the London Underground) as long as the original tiles are in good condition. Seal them with sealer primer so tiles will adhere, and remember that you'll need wooden lipping, or tile slivers, to conceal the double thickness at the top.

How many tiles?

You can work out the number of tiles you require by measuring the area and dividing it by the size of the tiles. Use the chart above as a ready reckoner, but remember that the sizes given only approximate to those of the most popular tiles, and that you'll need to add 10 per cent to allow for the inevitable breakages.

Equipment

You will need:
- a spirit level, to ensure that the tiles are on the true horizontal.
- a plumb bob and line (see page 36) to make sure they are on the true vertical.
- a wide-bladed scraper (see page 11) or trowel to apply adhesive.
- a tile cutter. Choose between one of the excellent commercial cutters, a wheeled cutter with jaws which grasp the tile or a simple tungsten carbide tipped cutter.
- pincers, to snip away small sections of tile when fitting round pipes and similar obstructions.
- a tile saw for cutting L-shaped tiles or other awkward shapes.
- a tile file for smoothing rough edges.
- a screwdriver and screws, or hammer and masonry nails, for attaching the supporting sticks.
- waterproof wall tile mastic adhesive: one gallon will cover approximately 50 square feet.
- grout, in powder form or ready-mixed. Epoxy grout is required when grouting worktops and waterproof grout when tiling around sinks, showers and baths. One pound covers about 18 square feet.

You'll also need a sponge to wipe away excess grout, a flexible sealant to form a watertight rim round windows, baths and sinks and straight sticks to act as guides.

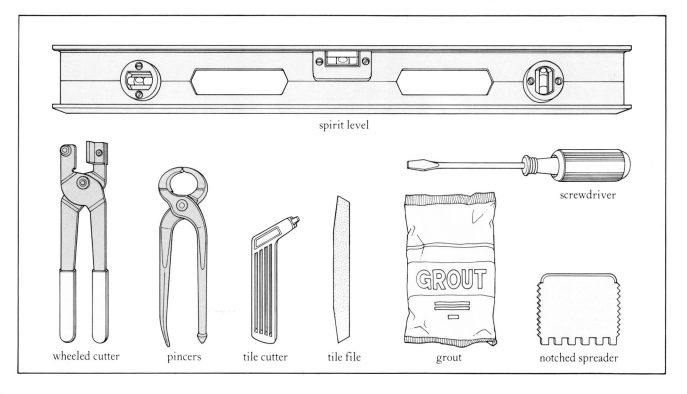

spirit level

wheeled cutter | pincers | tile cutter | tile file | grout | notched spreader

screwdriver

Tiling Techniques

The method described here is appropriate to large areas and does not apply to, say, one line of tiles used as a backsplash behind a basin. First you'll need to establish horizontal and vertical lines to make sure that the tiling is straight. Measure one tile up from the baseboard or worktop. Use the spirit level to work out the true horizontal and establish a vertical line using this or the plumb bob and line if easier. Draw pencil lines to mark these positions.

Attach a stick with screws or masonry nails, so that it butts up to the horizontal line. (It should extend right along the area to be tiled.) This will be your starting point.

Mark the centre of the stick. Using a tile as a measure, pencil the position of each tile on the stick. You'd normally start at the centre but if you realize that you will end up with a narrow gap at the end of the row, adjust your starting position to make cutting easier. Remember to allow for lugs or tile spacers in your calculations.

Attach a vertical stick to the wall to serve as a guide to the first row of vertical tiles. Corners, door frames and so on are seldom true so do not use these as starting points for tiling. Now you can begin.

Finishing and grouting

When all the tiles are in place, leave to dry for 48 hours (longer if you have used waterproof adhesive).

Press the grout into the gaps with a sponge. Wipe away the excess. Use a popsicle stick to neaten up the grout and leave to dry for 24 hours. If you're tiling a worktop, you'll find that epoxy grout is very stiff, so allow plenty of time for this stage. (An old toothbrush can be used to work it in.) Remember that you'll need to grout the exposed edge of universal tiles to protect them.

Polish the tiles with a soft cloth.

Fixing tiles

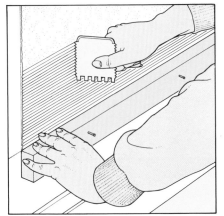

Spread the mastic on to a square yard of wall and comb it into ridges with the notched spreader. Aim for an even thickness.

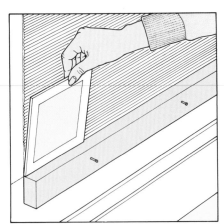

Position the first tile with a slight twist to bed it in. It should be placed snugly in the angle where the horizontal and vertical sticks meet. If you have to remove it, comb the mastic again.

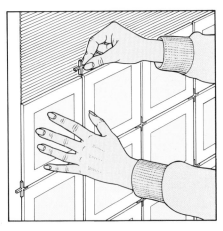

Place spacers or matchsticks at the top and bottom of a universal tile and position the next tile in the same way. Don't slide the tile into place or you'll create a build-up of mastic.

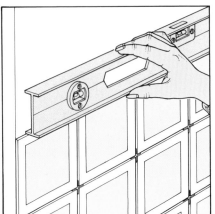

Continue until you reach the end of the wall, removing spacers every square yard, and checking the level from time to time. Work upwards, attaching all the whole tiles first. Then remove the stick and tackle the remaining space.

Cutting straight lines

With a tungsten carbide cutter . . . score the glazed surface of the tile along the line you want to cut using a ruler to ensure that you have a straight edge.

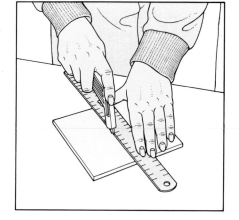

Place matchsticks or a pencil (depending on the thickness of the tile) beneath the scored line, and press firmly on both sides of the tile. It should separate cleanly.

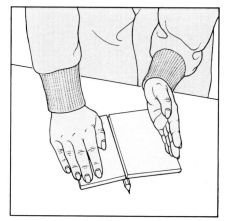

With a wheeled cutter . . . score the tile using the special wheel. Use a ruler again to make sure that the line is straight.

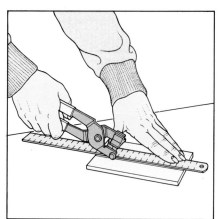

Then clasp the tile in the cutter's jaws and press the tile apart. Smooth the cut edges with a file. Apply adhesive direct to the back of the cut tile and press it into place.

Cutting tiles

It's a good idea to experiment with old tiles first to see which cutter you prefer and to master the technique.

Pincers will cope with small irregular shapes. Copy the shape on to a piece of card to make a template and use it to mark the tile. Score this pattern with a tile cutter and then nibble away at the tile with the pincers until you have the shape you require. If the area is large, score the tile in a criss-cross pattern to make it more friable.

Smooth the cut edges with a file. This technique works well for small areas; for large gaps it is often easier to join cut tiles. If you plan to do a lot of tiling, a tile saw is a good investment; the tile is held in a vise and the saw used to make a clean cut.

Use a template cut from cardboard, and mark the shape to be cut on the tile. Now score this with a tile cutter before nibbling away at the shape with pincers. Finish by smoothing with a tile file.

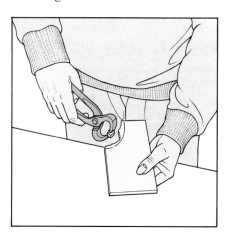

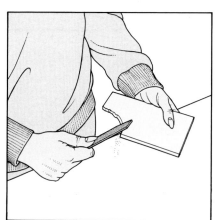

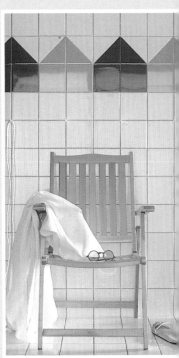

Tiling

A practical choice for walls, floors and even work surfaces, tiles look stylish and elegant, especially in kitchens and bathrooms. They are available in a wide range of shapes, sizes and materials and, suitably finished, form an easy-to-clean, hard-wearing surface. Although sometimes cold to the touch, tiles can form a waterproof, insulating layer.

Top left: in a predominantly grey bathroom with freestanding bath, beige and white border tiles are used to define mirror areas.

Top right: Edwardian-style blue and white tiles on walls and floor contribute to the clean and clinical atmosphere of this smart bathroom.

Bottom, far left: Spanish terracotta tiles with a high glaze finish frame a colourful mosaic of broken tiles arranged in a random design.

Bottom, left: despite the lack of windows this hall provides a bright welcome, with mirror tiles framing the doorway and reflecting the artificial light.

Bottom right: sitting under the fence? Chevrons of carefully cut ceramic tiles, rather reminiscent of a garden gate, give this room an outdoorsy feel.

Bottom, far right: as long as their colours are complementary, genuine Victorian tiles don't need to match to make a stunning display.

Ceilings

Wait before you reach for the white paint to decorate the ceiling. You can play tricks with perspective by using a deep colour to reduce the apparent height of a room, or a light one so that the ceiling seems to recede. Always start with the ceiling when you redecorate a room so that any runs are obliterated when you paint or paper the walls. Although the techniques are the same, it can be difficult to work above your head. This section shows how to make it easier by setting up a work station, with advice on how to paint or paper a ceiling and how to fix cornice and coving for a neat finish.

Related colours make the ceiling an integral part of the decor (right) but there's no need to keep to paint; timber adds warmth and conceals downlighters (below).

Whether you intend to paper or paint a room, you should always start with the ceiling so that the inevitable splashes and runs will be hidden when you cover the walls. However, it's best for beginners to get the hang of painting and papering techniques by practising on the walls first. Though it's not particularly difficult to decorate a ceiling, remember that gravity is working against you and that it's tiring to work for any length of time with your arms above your head.

Preparation

The first thing to do is to set up a stable work station. To save moving the steps every few minutes, use two stepstools linked by a plank. This will give you access to the ceiling and encourage an uninterrupted workflow – vital when papering a ceiling. Remove light fixtures and take up any carpet or protect it with plastic topped by a sheet, and take care to cover yourself. You'll need a scarf or cap for your hair and possibly goggles – especially advisable if you wear glasses – to prevent paint from spattering your face.

Prepare the ceiling by removing old wallpaper unless this adheres well and you intend to paint over it. Be sure to use latex paint in this instance, and make sure that the wallpaper is colorfast and won't bleed through the paint. Fill cracks and sand level in the usual way (see pages 14-15). Wash the ceiling with

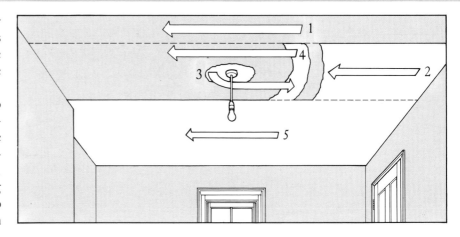

Work in yard-wide bands (1 and 5). Where there's a ceiling fixture start in the same way (2) but cut in round the rose (3) before returning to complete the band (4).

diluted detergent and then rinse. (A clean squeegee or window-cleaning tool makes light of this.) New plasterboard will need a priming coat of thinned latex paint; an old ceiling should be painted with stabilising solution if it is flaky.

Painting

Work across the ceiling in yard-wide stripes, cutting in at the perimeter and round the light (see pages 18-23). Rollers and paint pads are the easiest tools to use for the bulk of the job (except cutting in) but you can use also a brush, if you prefer. Brushes are more apt to leave marks where strips of paint overlap. This is especially true of alkyd paints, and as a result, latex paints are generally preferred. If you do opt for an alkyd paint, however, be sure not to paint in strips more than 2 feet wide, and

walk across the width rather than the length of the ceiling so you can start the next stripe of paint before the previous one dries, thus minimising any lap marks. Choose flat finish paint for plaster or plasterboard, semigloss if you want to highlight a textured ceiling. Remember that ceilings don't have to be white: a deep colour will seem to reduce the height of a high ceiling while a pastel will offset contrasting mouldings effectively.

Support a scaffold board by stepladder plus a stepstool. This makes decorating the ceiling infinitely easier, whether you paint or paper it. You'll need to be about 10 inches from the ceiling to give adequate headroom.

Papering

Papering a ceiling is easy – that is, if you're patient and determined, and have a co-operative partner. Otherwise you'd be well advised to keep to paint or to attempt only small areas like bathrooms and single bedrooms. Lining the ceiling is often the only way to achieve a smooth finish for paint, and all-over patterns are especially attractive in rooms where the wall surface is interrupted, such as in bathrooms and bedrooms with dormer windows. But where there are fewer breaks in the surface, the lengths of paper are unwieldy and difficult to manipulate. Determined to have a try? Then follow these instructions.

Calculate how much paper you will need, using the chart below.

Paper Calculator

Distance around ceiling	Standard single rolls
28–32 feet	2
33–44 feet	4
45–54 feet	6
55–64 feet	8
65–70 feet	10

Choose your wallcovering with care. Some heavy papers may not adhere properly and you may need a slightly stronger than normal adhesive, including fungicide if it is a washable vinyl paper, to keep the paper in place, so check for suitability with your supplier.

Decide whether you want to work along the room or across it. It's obviously easier to paste shorter lengths, but you may prefer the pattern to flow the other way. (Remember to hang lining paper in the opposite direction to the paper which goes over it.) Generally it is better to start papering adjacent to the main window and then to work backwards into the room.

1

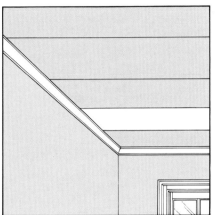

2

3

4

Papering a ceiling

Size the ceiling with diluted wallpaper paste. This makes the surface less absorbent. Mark a straight line on the ceiling to act as a guide. Measure the wallpaper and subtract 10 inches. Mark this distance from the wall at each end of the ceiling. Pin a length of chalked string to each mark and snap it against the ceiling. This gives you your starting point and allows for the paper to overlap on to the wall.

Hang the first length of wallpaper on the side of the line away from the wall. (It's best to start near the window and work away from the light.) Measure and cut all the lengths you'll need at the same time but don't paste too many at once; hanging them may take longer than you think. Paste the length of paper a little at a time and fold into a concertina, pasted edge to pasted edge, with even folds about a foot wide. (Remember to allow sufficient soaking time to prevent bubbles.)

Support the concertina on a spare roll of wallpaper. If the length of paper is not too long you should be able to cope by supporting it with the spare roll of paper while you gradually unfold it and brush it into place with a smoothing brush. If it's particularly heavy, ask a partner to support it with a broom while you work.

Allow a 1 inch overlap if you intend to paper the walls, otherwise trim wallpaper so that it fits snugly up to cornice or coving and slit the paper to accommodate a chimney breast or alcove. Butt join succeeding lengths and press the seams firmly with a seam roller unless the paper is embossed.

Papering around a light fixture

The trick here is to pretend the obstacle doesn't exist.

Paper up to the fixture and slit the paper slightly so that you can paste it down satisfactorily.

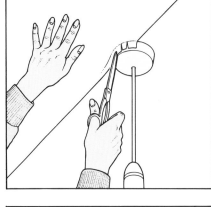

Continue hanging the next length as normal, butt-joining it to the previous one. Bring the paper up and over the light fixture. Now cut into this piece of paper so that it fits around the fixture.

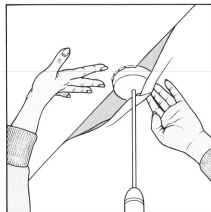

Brush the paper into place. Cut away the excess paper with a trimming knife, allowing a ¼ inch overlap.

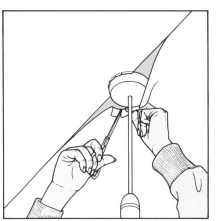

Turn off the electricity and remove the fixture cover. Tuck the overlap around the fixture and replace the cover. If the fixture happens to fall in the centre of the paper then make a hole and pull it through. Continue hanging the complete length before returning to trim the paper around the fixture as above.

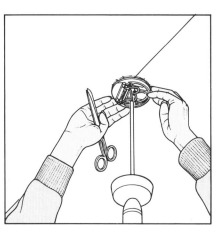

Cornices and coving

What's the difference? Both fit into the angle between wall and ceiling to provide a neat finish concealing wires – and cracks.

Cornices are ornamental and usually made from traditional products (plaster or wood) in traditional styles though convincing plastic varieties are available. Plaster cornice should be stuck down with contact adhesive, which sets as soon as the cornice is pressed into place, or with one recommended for wood panelling. Plastic resin and wood cornices need wood adhesive and wooden moulding will also require nails. This is a general guide; for the best results, follow the manufacturer's instructions.

Coving is plain and made from gypsum or wood. Coving is lighter than cornice and easier to handle.

Whichever you decide to use, you will need to remove all wallpaper from the area it will cover and ensure that the wall is clean and dry so that the cornice or coving adheres properly. Make a note of the internal and external angles – cutting the wrong way will waste material!

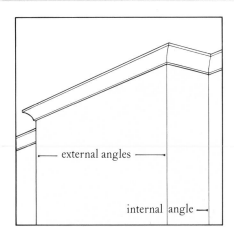

external angles

internal angle

Finish the area by sanding slightly so the adhesive will adhere.

Equipment

To install gypsum coving you will need:

- a mitre box, unless a paper template is provided with the cove.
- a tenon saw.
- sandpaper.
- a filling knife.
- a damp sponge.
- the correct adhesive.

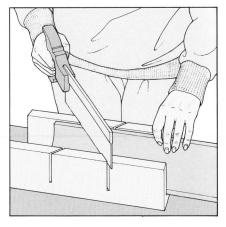

1

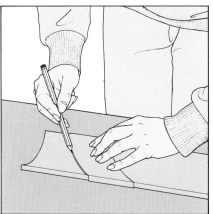

2

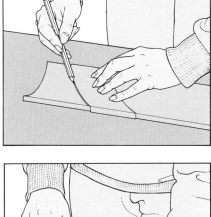

3

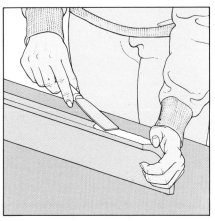

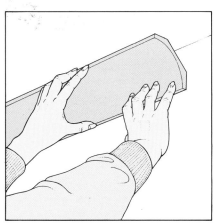

4

Installing gypsum coving

Measure the room to work out the lengths you will need.

With a mitre box or a paper template, cut the coving with the angles you require. Sand the edges lightly until smooth.

With a new paper template you will need to mark the cutting line in pencil before sawing carefully along the line.

Apply adhesive on to the back and attaching edges of the coving. 'Butter' it generously with a filling knife but try not to smear the surface.

Hold it up to the wall, and when it is in position press it into place.

If it's particularly heavy, secure with nails above and below the cove edges – do not nail through the cove. Remove excess adhesive with a sponge before it sets.

Woodwork & Furniture

How do you choose between paint and varnish?
How can you achieve a perfect glossy finish?
What's the best way to strip wood? And exactly
how do people manage to turn those tatty-looking
junk shop finds into elegant period furniture?
Read on to discover the tricks of the trade,
whether you're painting structural woodwork like
window frames, doors and baseboards, renovating
old furniture, tackling an unusual type of surface
— or personalising particle board.

*A light and airy kitchen with beautiful wood surfaces echoes
the tones and textures of the natural world, and makes the
most of a wonderful view with sliding glass doors (right).
Alternatively, wood panelling can be painted and a cane
chair and bamboo table turned into perfect partners with a
coat of eggshell paint (below).*

How can you achieve the perfect glossy finish that you see in so many advertisements? Some skill in applying the paint is, of course, essential but it's the preparation that's really important. This is because the topcoat will probably be a reflective solvent-based paint or varnish which shows up every bump.

Preparing to . . . paint

The good news is that if the old paintwork is sound, relatively free from knocks or sap seeping through from untreated knots, all you have to do is to sand it smooth and wash it down. Existing paintwork in good condition provides the perfect base for the new coat so don't attempt to remove it unless it's really necessary. Make sure you don't skimp on the cleaning process; wash with diluted detergent or TSP solution, rinse and allow to dry. Take particular care in corners where dirt builds up and with window frames where it's worth cleaning the outside too, especially when painting sash windows. If the paintwork is in a mostly fair condition but poor in parts, you can spot-treat it, filling where necessary, building it up with primer and sanding it level.

Preparing to . . . varnish

Varnish is transparent so it will show every flaw. You'll have to strip existing paint and you may have to stain or bleach the wood and use a coloured filler to obtain a uniform effect. Pine is the only softwood that's regularly stripped and varnished, for varnish is usually reserved for more expensive hardwoods so that the beauty of the grain will show through. Think hard before you decide to varnish furniture or woodwork currently covered by paint. Not only will you need to strip it completely, you must also be prepared to find patched and filled areas, concealed by paint, which will be hard to hide beneath transparent varnish, however well applied.

Stripping paint

The three ways to strip paint are:
. . .dry stripping.
. . .with chemicals (liquid, gel or paste).
. . .with heat (using a propane or blow torch or an electric paint softener or remover).

Equipment

In addition to the tools mentioned above you will also need:
● a scraper or stripping knife to lift off the paint.
● shavehooks for working in corners. The two common types are the triangular shape and the combination shavehook with both curved and straight edges.
● steel wool for scouring intricate areas.

Dry stripping

This quite simply involves slipping a scraper behind layers of flaking paint to pull them away. It is inevitably a rough and ready method and must be followed by sanding. You can also remove paint by sanding alone. Hand-sanding is hard going but produces a fine finish. Alternatively you can use an electrically powered sander or a drill attachment – see page 60.

Chemical stripping

Chemicals are the best choice for elaborate mouldings, banisters, turned furniture and other complicated pieces. You'll need patience; some chemical strippers will remove only one layer at a time and you must allow anything from 15 to 20 minutes for the chemical to penetrate and soften the paint. Apply with a wooden paintbrush (an artist's brush is best for tricky areas) and strip with a scraper or stiff brush before cleaning with water or paint thinner, according to the manufacturer's instructions, to neutralise the chemical. You may need a special stripper for varnish though many stripping solutions are dual-purpose – check on the label. Shellac, or French polish, can be removed with general purpose furniture restorer or denatured alcohol rubbed on with steel wool. Wipe the shellac off with a rag and finish with dry steel wool, working along the grain.

Remember to wear rubber gloves as chemicals are caustic. Use only in well-ventilated rooms (or outside) and put down plenty of newspaper to collect the mess. Stand chair and table legs in saucers to catch surplus stripper for re-use and be prepared to re-apply the chemical three times to remove stubborn layers of paint.

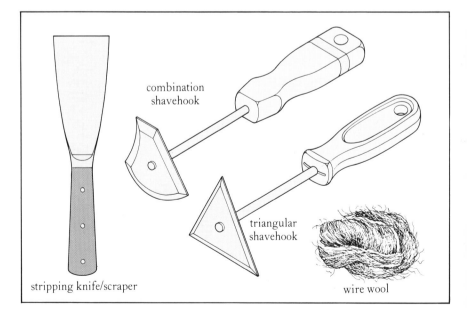

combination shavehook

triangular shavehook

stripping knife/scraper

wire wool

Heat stripping

Heat stripping is fast but it can be hazardous. It's often difficult to achieve a fine finish, so you may want to reserve this method for large, straightforward areas, or for furniture or woodwork which is to be re-painted.

Electric paint removers have made this method of stripping infinitely safer. They are less likely to scorch the wood — a common hazard with propane and blowtorches that use a naked flame. An electric paint remover may take longer, but it is simple to use. You can buy models with variable heat controls to increase or turn down the power.

Blowtorches were the original aid to heat stripping and run on gas. They need to be primed and warmed and can be unpredictable to use as the flame may flare unexpectedly, so take adequate safety precautions.

Make sure you wear gloves (gardening gloves are ideal) when using a blowtorch and hold it 8 inches away from the wood, taking care not to scorch the wood or, worse, set fire to it.

All methods of heat stripping work well on solvent-based paints. Move the electric paint remover or blowtorch with one hand while removing layers of paint with a scraper held in the other. Work upwards from the bottom so the hot air softens successive areas of paint. Shield windows from direct heat as the putty may melt and the glass may crack if exposed to its force. Remember to wear goggles when working high up on picture rails or window frames so that burning paint doesn't fall in your eyes. Don't forget to protect the floor from being scorched by hot scrapings, but use a non-flammable material, not newspaper! Remember to remove all soft furnishings and carpets, before you start.

1

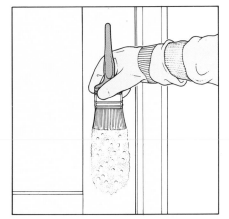

2

3

4

Stripping wood

Apply chemical stripper with a paintbrush and allow sufficient time for the solvent to penetrate and soften the paint before you start to scrape it off. Paste stripper may be easier to use on elaborate mouldings.

Hold an electric paint remover in one hand while you ease the softened paint away with a scraper held in the other. Start from the bottom and work upwards to take advantage of the heat rising.

A blow torch with a flame spreader maximises its effect. Take care not to hold it too close to the wood or it may scorch or burn.

A blow torch with a concentrated flame is ideal for stubborn areas. Always work from the bottom up and remember to wear gloves to protect your hands.

Sanding

Hand-sanding completes the stripping process. It's certainly possible to strip paint in this way, starting with coarse abrasive paper and finishing with fine, but it can be a laborious process – it's usually best to reserve hand-sanding for the final stage. Use a sanding block made from wood, cork or rubber, with the appropriate grade of abrasive paper. Though expensive, silicon carbide paper is a good choice as it can be used wet or dry.

A disc sander attached to a drill will remove paint but may well score the surface of the wood. Reserve it for rough work.

An orbital sander is so called because the abrasive in the paper clipped to the sole plate moves in small circles when vibrated. This is also called a finishing sander and it's ideal for achieving a fine finish over a large area. You may have to finish corners by hand and although orbital sanders take the hard work out of sanding they are not particularly fast. Some models have dust-bags to cut down the mess.

A belt sander is necessary for sanding at speed. It's larger and more powerful than an orbital so it will strip paint and sand floors, but it won't give a fine finish and is best used for large-scale projects.

Liquid sander is a solvent, designed to soften the top layer of paint before you redecorate. It's applied with a sponge, wiped off with a wet cloth

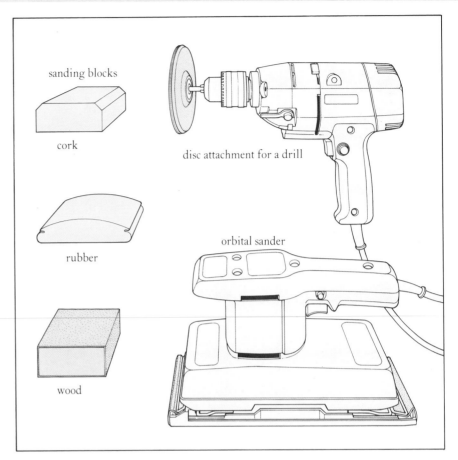

sanding blocks

cork

disc attachment for a drill

rubber

orbital sander

wood

and left to dry thoroughly before repainting.

When using a sanding block, an orbital or belt sander always sand along the grain (see below left). The revolving movement of a disc sander makes this impossible – that's why you won't achieve a smooth effect. It's particularly important to follow the grain if you intend to varnish, as scratches across the wood will be magnified by the clear finish. When the wood is sanded to your satisfaction, wipe it down with a rag wrung out with paint thinner to remove traces of dust before you paint or varnish.

Knotting

Resin from knots in the wood will seep through and stain unless they are sealed. Use shellac-based knotting solution, applied with an artist's paintbrush (right) to cover the knots in bare wood before you apply primer. Apply two coats of the solution, allowing time to dry in

between. Then use aluminium primer on that area before adding undercoat and topcoat.

If knots have stained existing paintwork you can strip the paint completely. Heat stripping back to the bare wood, on doors or window frames for example, tends to draw out the resin and encourages the wood to dry out. Apply knotting solution before repainting. Alternatively, try touching in the stain with aluminium primer/sealer.

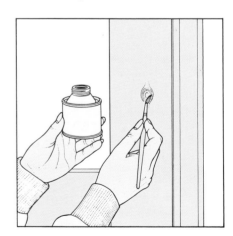

Wooden floors look good from the word 'go', yet improve with age.

Filling

Multi-purpose filler in powder form or ready-mixed can be used to pack dents and to coat the ends of particle boards like chipboard which absorb paint too quickly for a fine finish. Allow to dry and sand level before applying primer.

Wood filler is designed to blend with natural wood and to flex as it expands and contracts. Mix with wood dye for an exact match when varnishing. Special wax crayons in various wood shades are available for dealing with scratches.

Priming

Primer is essential groundwork when painting wood. It's not always necessary to buy special wood primer unless you prefer because it's possible to use 'universal' primer on wood, plaster and metal. Don't ignore the one rule that still holds – always use primer on bare wood. Primer seals the wood to prevent it from absorbing paint and helps the next coat adhere. Without it, wood saps and resins may seep through the paint.

Water-based primer (quick drying primer or primer/undercoat) dries quickly (allow two hours before over-painting) and doubles as an undercoat. It contains acrylic resins for protection but it is not as hard-wearing as solvent-based primer and cannot be used outside.

Solvent- or oil-based primer is available in grey or white for inside and outside use. Work it well into the grain and allow to dry for at least 12 hours before applying the next coat.

Aluminium primer is water-resistant and is recommended for any area where water is likely to collect. For complete protection it's a good idea to apply an initial coat of primer thinned with 10 per cent paint thinner.

Ask the Professionals

Q How should I strip the banisters and stair rail in my Victorian house?

A *Try a combination of methods. Chemical stripper and hand-sanding is usually the most effective but you could try softening the paint with an electric paint remover in accessible areas, taking care not to scorch the wood. Paste stripper is easy to apply and should cling to the banisters so there's less waste than with liquid or gel types. Keep the paste moist by watering with a plant sprayer when possible. Remove with a scrubbing brush and steel wool (an old toothbrush is useful too) and sand down with silicon carbide or fine grade sandpaper to finish.*

Q How can I remove layers of wax from an old dining table?

A *To strip back to bare wood, choose a dual-purpose paint and varnish remover which will also disperse the wax. If you want to preserve the finish, use paint thinner rubbed in with steel wool, working along the grain. Wash down with dilute detergent solution and rinse, but don't overwet the wood.*

Q Can I use a belt sander on doors and baseboards? I find manual sanding tedious and orbitals rather slow.

A *A belt sander is perfect for speedy, rough work, but don't use it on decorative baseboards or doors with mouldings. Use the finest grade of abrasive paper you can find to fit the machine – that way you should obtain a finish fine enough for repainting. If you intend to varnish, complete by sanding down by hand.*

Paints and varnishes

When you consider the punishment woodwork receives, you'll realize why it's usual to protect it with a hard-wearing solvent-based paint. Furniture, doors and window frames have to sustain constant use, while baseboards are specifically designed to take the knocks that would damage the walls; all need regular cleaning to remove fingerprints and scuff marks. Usually flat paint is reserved for walls and semigloss or gloss used on woodwork; However, some people prefer to use all semigloss or all flat paint for walls and woodwork depending on the taste of the individuals involved. Clear varnish, in various degrees of sheen, provides a transparent protective layer and allows the wood to show through, while tinted varnish or wood stain will change its colour. You can even use flat latex paint if you prefer, provided you coat it with clear varnish to prevent chips and scratches.

Paint

Cellulose-based spray paint is intended for touching in scratches on cars. It has a restricted role in the home, but you may find it useful for spraying plastics or metal. It can't be used over gloss or eggshell so you will have to remove these completely before you begin.

Latex semigloss enamel has an attractive 'mid-sheen' finish. It is easy to use and clean up (it is thinned and cleaned up with water) and is versatile and reasonably durable, although not as rugged as solvent-based gloss paint.

Alkyd semigloss is similar to latex semigloss but is thinned and cleaned up with paint thinner and tends to be a bit more durable.

Enamel has a hard, shiny finish. It may contain metallic pigment, needs no undercoat or primer and protects against rust. It's expensive, so it is sold in small cans and used for painting limited areas of wood or metal.

Flat alkyd or latex paint absorbs grease and marks easily, so it should be sealed with clear varnish if used on woodwork.

Alkyd gloss paint may be thixotropic (non-drip) or liquid. Non-drip gloss is designed to cover in one coat, though if you're changing from a very dark to a light colour you may need to use two. Liquid gloss is the last step in the traditional paint used on woodwork, although semigloss is widely used as well. For a quality finish you may need to use two coats of liquid gloss paint. The two types of gloss paint should be applied differently (see painting techniques on page 65) and have contrasting characteristics. Non-drip gloss won't run but tends to show brush marks while liquid gloss sags if brushed on too thickly but has a mirror finish if correctly applied.

Lacquer can be a high-gloss paint or a clear varnish. It is available in both spray and brush-on varieties and dries very rapidly. It should never be used over existing paint, as it tends to dissolve it.

Varnish

Polyurethane varnish is the type most commonly used today. There's a choice of finishes from matt and semigloss to gloss, also called hard glaze, and diamond finish. (Some matt and semigloss finishes offer less protection than high gloss, so check before you buy. This is especially important when buying varnish to act as a floor sealer.) Most varnish is used straight from the can, but two-step products, which involve mixing separate components, may be used to achieve a very hard finish. Varnish may be clear or coloured. Pre-mixed wood colours such as dark oak or walnut are the

Coverage and Drying Times (coverage varies with product and absorbency of wood)

Type of paint	Area covered per litre	Touch dry (in hours)	Recoatable (in hours)
eggshell	15sq m	12	16
enamel	10sq m	2-3	16
flat oil paint	15sq m	6	12
gloss (liquid)	17sq m	12	16
gloss (non-drip)	12-14sq m	1-3	(one coat product)
lacquer	12-14sq m	2	6
microporous paint	12-14sq m	3	(one coat product)
polyurethane varnish	16-17sq m	3	16-24
primer (aluminium)	15sq m	2	6
primer (solvent based)	12sq m	4	12
primer (water based)	12sq m	1	2-4
solvent-based silk finish/sheen	11sq m	12	16
undercoat	15sq m	8	12
wood stain	20-30sq m	½-3	16

most popular, but it's also possible to tint varnish using a manufacturer's paint mixing system. This gives you a wide range of colours but care is needed to avoid runs during application. Remember that tinted varnish won't give you the same depth of colour as wood stain topped by clear varnish, and that chips will be more obvious because the natural wood beneath will show through.

Shellac (button polish) is a natural product used in French polishing and knotting fluid. It's best thought of as a hard-wearing polish rather than as a sealer because it is not impermeable; water stains and ring marks are a particular problem so it's best reserved for decorative areas rather than used on table or cupboard tops.

Wood bleach allows you to apply a light stain on a dark wood. It's also useful for obliterating dark patches on newly stripped wood.

Wood stain may be based on water, solvent or alcohol. Water-based stains are often bought in powder form and give the brightest colour. Solvent-based stains are more transparent and dry slowly; alcohol-based stains are midway between the two in effect and are quick to dry.

Furniture can be stripped right down and stained to bring out the natural beauty of the wood, but must be well sealed to withstand everyday wear and tear.

Sequence of painting

Decorate a room in this order so that drips do not spoil the finish: if you are painting the walls, tackle the ceiling, then walls and finally woodwork. When using wallpaper, first paint the ceiling, then the woodwork, before you wallpaper.

Woodwork should be tackled systematically too: treat windows first, then doors and then baseboards.

Paint banisters and stair rail before stairs. If you intend to paint or varnish an entire staircase, treat alternate treads to allow access.

Remember to remove all door and window 'furniture' to make painting easier and to prevent runs.

Equipment

For painting you will need:
● a cutting-in brush or paint pad for glazing bars and mouldings.
● a 1 inch brush for window and door frames.
● 2 and 3 inch brushes for baseboards and doors.
● a paint shield or masking tape to protect windows, walls and floorings. The paint film should cover the window pane by ⅛ inch so that it prevents moisture from the pane from seeping into the wood.
● a stick for stirring the paint.
● an opener for paint tins.
● a home-made tack rag or lint-free rag moistened with paint thinner for removing dust specks.
● a paint bucket if you're using paint from a gallon can.
For varnishing you will need:
● a varnish brush 1 or 2 inches wide. This has more bristles to help smooth out the varnish.
● or a new good quality paintbrush. Never use a brush that you've used for paint because pieces of pigment will cloud the varnish.

Buy a can of paint thinner for cleaning brushes and erasing mistakes. Some non-drip gloss can be washed out with diluted detergent and water, but in most cases solvent-

based paint and varnish should be cleaned and thinned with the appropriate solvent. In 90 percent of cases that's paint thinner, but cellulose-based spray paint should be cleaned with acetone (nail varnish remover) and special thinners used for some enamels. Shellac should be removed with denatured alcohol.

Painting techniques

Alkyd gloss and semigloss are trickier to use than latex. That's because they are less absorbent and, as they're reflective, magnify mistakes.

Skilfully bambooed furniture is highlighted by plain yet sunny walls.

Make sure that the surface to be painted is completely smooth and clean and take care not to overload the brush when using gloss or semigloss or to overbrush when using non-drip paint.

With gloss and semigloss, dip the brush in the paint until one-third of the bristle area is covered and press the bristles against the side of the can to remove excess paint. Don't wipe

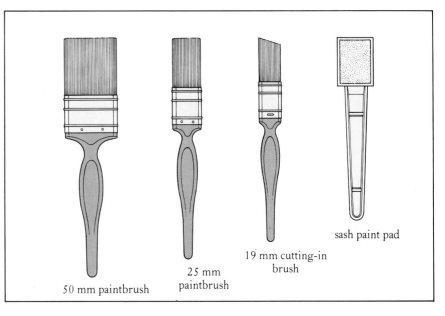

50 mm paintbrush

25 mm paintbrush

19 mm cutting-in brush

sash paint pad

the bristles on the rim as the residue may dry out and drop into the paint below.

Hold a small brush like a pencil, a wide one by the stock. Work along the grain (or the longest edge when painting particle board) and away from the light if possible, applying the paint in parallel strips. Apply the paint with the grain, then brush upwards and, finally, with the grain. Then reload the brush and paint the adjacent strip. Now spread the paint across the grain to join the two strips. 'Lay off' with feather-like strokes towards the light to prevent brush marks.

With non-drip gloss, dip the brush into the paint as above but do not wipe against the side of the can – non-drip paint should be applied generously.

Dot patches of paint in a line along the grain or longest edge, working away from the light if you can. Cover a small area at a time.

Connect the patches with a sweeping stroke, then brush back and forth across the grain. Lay off in the first direction, towards the light.

With both liquid and non-drip gloss, try to apply the paint more thinly at the edge of each band to avoid a build-up of paint.

Varnishing techniques

Apply an initial coat of varnish thinned with 10 percent paint thinner on bare wood, then sand down and clean, or sand and clean existing varnish or wood stain.

Dip the brush into the can so that half the bristle area is covered. Brush in long even strokes, working with the grain.

Brush out in the opposite direction from the wet edge, taking care to erase overlaps and brush marks.

Finish by brushing in the first direction in one smooth stroke. You'll need two or three coats of varnish for a good finish. Allow to dry, then sand with extra-fine steel wool and clean between each coat.

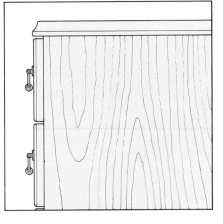

1

2

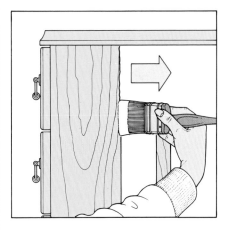

3

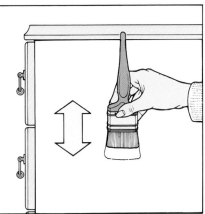

4

Applying alkyd gloss paint

It's important to work with the grain when painting woodwork to obtain the best results. If you're painting particle board, which has no grain, work away from the light instead.

When using alkyd gloss paint, apply the paint in parallel strips with a flowing down and then up movement to disperse the paint evenly and to prevent drips. (You'll find it easier to daub non-drip gloss on in patches before joining them up, to avoid over-brushing.) Reload the brush before painting each strip.

Without reloading the brush, spread the paint across to join the two strips, working against the grain. This is the technique to use whether you're applying liquid or non-drip gloss. It distributes the paint over the surface to give even coverage.

'Lay off' with feather-light strokes along the grain for a fine finish and to eliminate brushmarks. Work toward the light when painting particle board for a similar effect.

Ask the Professionals

Q What should I use to paint a second-hand crib? I'm worried about the lead content.

A *Federal regulations have prohibited lead in house paints for many years, so unless the crib itself is very old and was originally painted with a lead based paint, lead isn't apt to be a problem. Take special care when stripping paint in old houses as pre-war paint contained a high proportion of lead. Don't use a power sander which raises the dust or a blowtorch which may draw out poisonous fumes. Choose between silicon carbide paper used wet, chemical stripper or an electric paint remover, and always work in a well-ventilated room.*

Q Which gives better results – liquid or non-drip gloss?

A *If you paint to professional standards, choose liquid gloss it should give a highly reflective smooth finish. It's important not to overload the brush to avoid drips and runs. Beginners may find liquid gloss difficult to handle on vertical surfaces. Non-drip or thixotropic gloss has a gel-like consistency. One coat is usually all that's necessary, but two layers will be needed if there's a marked change of colour. Load the brush generously when using non-drip gloss and don't over-brush or you'll get insufficient coverage. It's difficult to avoid brush marks when using non-drip gloss so you might like to start with this and then progress to liquid gloss when more proficient.*

Q I want to varnish my pine kitchen units and change their colour (to green) at the same time. Should I choose coloured varnish or a wood stain with clear varnish on top?

A *That depends on the degree of colour change you want. If you're thinking of substantially altering the colour, opt for a wood stain plus clear varnish. Remember that water-based dyes give the brightest effect (you can use ordinary powder dye if you wish) though as they will raise the grain you will need to sand the wood before varnishing. If you want a slight colour change or a transparent watery effect, choose tinted varnish. Take special care when applying this as any overlaps or runs will be obvious.*

Q Can I paint over varnish?

A *Not recommended – but you can varnish over paint! Just remember that when the time comes to redecorate you will need to remove the varnish again.*

Q What can I do about brown streaks bleeding through the surface of a newly painted door?

A *This is probably resin from untreated knots. If the door is badly affected, strip it to the bare wood. (Heat stripping will encourage the wood to dry out.) Treat the knots with two coats of knotting solution and paint the door with aluminium primer plus undercoat and top coat. If the patches are small, try sanding down and applying aluminium primer to individual areas before repainting.*

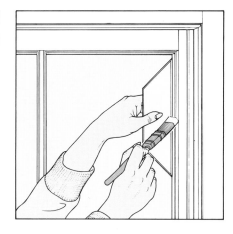

A paint shield is useful when painting windows to prevent paint from smudging the glass. Use a narrow (¾ or 1 inch) brush held by the handle like a pencil.

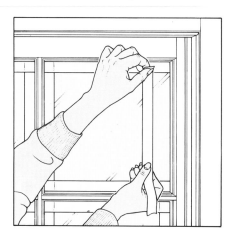

For fiddly areas it may be better to use masking tape. Remove it as soon as the paint is dry so that you don't pull the paint away with the tape.

Painting windows

Casement windows are uncomplicated unless they have a lot of small panes. In this case paint the inside edges (rebates) first, followed by the crossbars. The next step for all casement windows is to paint the top and bottom horizontals, the sides and edges and finally, the frame.

Sash windows are especially awkward because you can't reach every part at once. Paint them in this way.

1. Move the bottom sash up and the top sash down until they overlap by about 20 cm. Paint the bottom of the top sash.

2. Push the bottom sash down and

grasp the unpainted part of the top sash to pull it up so the window is almost closed. Now paint the rest of the top sash.

3. Paint the bottom sash and leave the window to dry. Insert matchsticks or pieces of cardboard to prevent the sashes from sticking together.

4. Paint the frame.

5. When the paint is dry, close the window completely and paint the remaining areas and the sill. Don't paint the sash cords or they'll stick.

Remember that you will have to repeat this procedure several times if you have stripped the wood as you will need to apply primer and top coats. Sand down lightly between coats and don't be tempted to skip any of the steps.

Painting doors

It's usual to paint the edge of the door to match the woodwork in the room in which it opens, so that you aren't faced by a contrasting strip. If you have a lot of doors to paint or

you want a fine finish using varnish or gloss paint, it's often worth taking the door off its hinges and laying it flat. Remember to do this if you are painting a new, untreated door so that you can paint and protect the bottom edge.

Panelled doors should be painted in the following order: 1. mouldings 2. panels 3. central verticals (muntins) 4. top and bottom horizontals 5. sides, edges and frame

1. paint the bottom of the top sash

2. paint the rest of the top sash

3. paint the bottom sash

4. paint the frame

5. paint the runners and sill

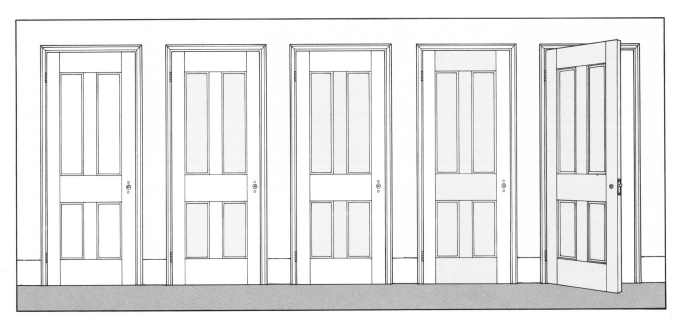

1. mouldings

2. panels

3. central verticals (muntins)

4. horizontals

5. sides, edges and frame

Painted Doors

When is a door not a door? When it's painted rainbow bright or dressed up to look like a classical archway, of course! Doors can make any room more interesting, adding pattern to a plain wall, serving as a base for a clever trompe l'oeil design, perhaps, or simply adding a bright splash of colour, so don't neglect them when planning your paint treatments.

Top left: add a hint of the gypsy caravan to an interior with clever stencils on a background of dark green to match the door frame.

Top right: concealed lighting set into the door frames shows up an adventurous use of colour, mock columns and arches adding a humorous touch.

Bottom, far left: a sophisticated high-tech interior is reflected in a flawless finish. Choose handles carefully to suit a room's style.

Bottom left: step into the blue yonder through this bold and brilliant mural, designed to brighten up the dullest of days.

Bottom right: door panels edged in a delicate salmon pink pick up the colour of walls and soft furnishings and the geometric pattern of the rug.

Bottom, far right: a Mondrian-inspired doorway wittily sets off a favourite picture against a background of dazzling white walls.

Preparing and repairing furniture

Painting or varnishing furniture gives it a new lease of life. It's more fun than painting structural woodwork and gives greater scope for decorative ideas. You'll find information on advanced techniques in the second half of this book, but first, here's how to renovate old furniture and prepare new to make it ready for painting.

Equipment

You will need:
- a scraper to remove wax and varnish to give a smooth finish.
- a plane (see page 80) for shaping wood.
- a file for smoothing edges.
- a chisel for cutting holes.
- a hammer (choose between a cross-peen hammer, with a ball at one end of the head and a straight edge at the other, and a claw hammer, handy for pulling out nails as well as driving them in).
- a wooden mallet.
- a saw.
- a drill plus attachments.
- a blade and holder.
- clamps to keep pieces in place when gluing.

Restoring old furniture

Don't attempt to renovate or decorate valuable furniture – you may do more harm than good.

Examine pieces for woodworm – its characteristic is numerous tiny pinholes. If you find it, treat it with commercial woodworm solution before you bring it into the house, otherwise your bargain may turn out to be far more costly than you at first anticipated.

Avoid furniture with large cracks or peeling veneer which requires

Even the tattiest junk shop find can be restored to its former glory for very little expense.

extensive repair, or furniture which has been badly mended.

Cleaning

The first step is to examine what's underneath the layers of grime, paint or varnish.

If the piece is merely dirty, wipe it down with diluted detergent and rinse. (Don't overwet wood or you'll raise the grain.) Bamboo should be sponged with a solution of soap flakes, water and borax and rinsed with warm salt water; unvarnished cane can be wiped with water and laundry detergent.

If it's covered in shellac or button polish, remove with general purpose furniture restorer or denatured alcohol and steel wool.

If it has been painted or varnished, strip the finish by sanding, by heat or with chemicals (see pages 58-60). Don't use a blowtorch on mouldings or if you intend to varnish the furniture later – heat can cause scorch marks in the wood.

Repairing

Chair rails and stretchers are subject to stress. If loose, try gluing and clamping. If they are broken, you'll need to replace them. Look in second-hand shops and architectural salvage firms for spare rails or stretchers which suit the style of the chair and can be planed to fit the fixing holes. Saw off the remains of the old rail and drill out the holes. Plane the new rail to fit and apply woodworking adhesive both to the tips of the rail and the holes. (Make sure you remove any animal glue left in the holes or the rail won't stick.) Fix in place and secure with clamps, then finish by staining or painting to match the rest.

Drawers often stick because they're distorted by damp. Chalk the edges and then close the drawer as best you can. When you open the drawer, the missing chalk marks will show you where it sticks. You can then sand or plane the affected areas. Seal the drawer to prevent the problem from

recurring and spray with furniture polish to ease its running. If the bottom of the drawer has warped, you may have to fit a new base, and if the runners are broken you'll need to replace them.

Hinges and castors won't work if the screw holes have become enlarged. Filler isn't strong enough to withstand the constant movement, so either replace existing screws with thicker screws or insert wall plugs in the holes before reattaching the existing screws.

Joints on tables and chairs often work loose when the dowels fracture. Unscrew the block and bang it with a mallet to sever the adhesive. Drill out the holes and fit new dowels ¼ inch shorter than the length of the holes they will fit. Nick a groove along the dowel, fill with woodworking adhesive and place in position on the block before refitting. Give the block a tap with the mallet to coax it into place.

Mouldings may be broken. Lumber yards stock a wide range so you may be able to replace the damaged part; it's also possible to have mouldings copied to order. Try not to patch moulding — it's better to replace a complete length — but if you do, remember to mitre the edges to fit.

Table legs which are wobbly can be levelled by cutting them all to the length of the shortest or by building the odd one up. Glue and screw the extra piece in place for strength and stability. Cracks in table tops can be stopped with a mixture of wood filler and epoxy resin glue, sanded down.

New furniture presents different problems. Particle boards (blockboard, chipboard and hardboard) have no grain and careful painting is required or brush marks will show when they are gloss-painted. The edges are more absorbent than the face, so to achieve an even finish coat with multi-purpose filler and sand smooth before painting.

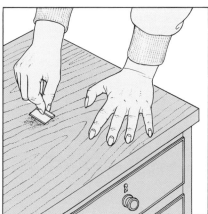

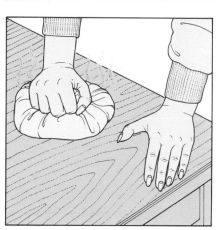

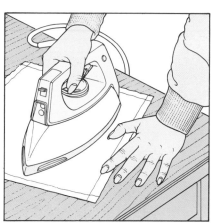

Surface repairs

You can conceal many scratches with wax crayon or shoe polish. On shellac or French polish, thin the scratch with denatured alcohol then build up with more shellac (see left) and sand level with silicon carbide paper. On other surfaces, try sanding scratches or use a mildly abrasive metal polish. Deep scratches should be filled with wood filler, sanded when dry.

Burns that have not penetrated beneath the surface will be removed when this is stripped away. For deeper burns, or to spot-treat marks, you'll need to cut away the area with a razor blade (left) and sand with fine abrasive paper. Use wood filler if the damage is extensive or build up with several layers of varnish.

Deep dents need to be filled but small ones may respond to heat treatment. First remove any protective finish so that the water can expand the wood. Place a wad of cotton in a dish towel and soak it in boiling water. Wring out slightly and press on to the dent (left), leaving it for several minutes. Eventually the wood should swell to obliterate the dent. As this treatment will mark the wood, sand and stain the area to match the surround.

Veneer blisters when damp. Try treating by ironing the blisters over a dish towel and leave for several days to see if they subside. If this doesn't work, slit the bubbles and glue flat.

Special Surfaces

Paint will cover more than just walls and woodwork, but sometimes you may have to look beyond the usual housepaints. These are fine for everyday use – you can use even fragile flat latex on floors, stairs and furniture with a few coats of polyurethane varnish for protection. But if you want to paint surfaces such as fabric, a fireplace or metal, you will need a special paint to suit specific requirements.

Appliances, like the range and refrigerator, are ideal subjects for enamel. With many varieties you don't even need to use a primer. With others, it's recommended that you apply the appropriate primer first (usually zinc chromate for metal, an aluminium, solvent- or water-based type for wood) so read the instructions carefully. Along with black and white, smooth enamel is available in a range of cheerful colours – ideal for brightening up the home. It can prove to be a useful product which provides the answer to many painting problems. Give the washing machine and refrigerator a fresh coat of white enamel, or brighten them up with red, green, yellow or blue. You can revive tired kitchen cupboards and disguise tiles with it, and use what's left in the can for painting china and glass to match. Use heat-resistant enamel on stoves, radiators and choose between smooth finishes and hammered effects (which pickle when applied) for a shiny, hard-wearing finish inside and outside the home. (Smooth enamel is a super-gloss; hammered finishes may contain metal particles for greater durability.)

Baths may be renewed by firms that specialize in re-enameling bathroom fixtures. These use acrylic finishes that are less durable than the original porcelain but are an ideal solution if you want to change the colour of your bathroom features but aren't prepared to invest in entirely new ones.

Children's rooms can be painted with latex semigloss paint. Because this is water-based, clean up and application are a breeze, and the semigloss finish is especially forgiving when it comes to dirt and stains. It has the added advantage of being available in an array of colours, which makes for imaginative decorative schemes that appeal to children.

China and glass can be decorated with enamel paint. Make sure the piece is perfectly clean and dry before you start. Don't expect the finish to withstand repeated washing, as it is applied over the glaze and is therefore unprotected.

Fabric can be transformed with dyes that are sprayed or painted on to the surface, then fixed by heat from a warm iron. Follow the manufacturer's washing instructions carefully, as the dyes may not be fast above 104°F.

Grates and fire-backs need heat-resistant paint such as stove or furnace black, which withstands temperatures of up to 400°F. It's usually necessary to give two coats, and the surface should be painted

Above: This splendid old radiator is painted with a special enamel that discolours less quickly than gloss paint.

Right: Kitchen cabinets, furniture and appliances can all be protected with hard-wearing, shiny enamel.

while cold.

Floorboards can be painted with anything from latex to undercoat as long as they are finished with several coats of varnish. You can use alkyd gloss paint alone, but restrict it to areas of light wear as it tends to chip. For concrete, consider special floor paint, which can also be used on wood, brick and stone. This treatment is similar to the type used in factories but here your colour choice isn't confined to dark green or brown – white, black, grey, blue, cream and red are also available. It's particularly useful for cellar, kitchen and conservatory floors, and ideal for playrooms, where you can create mini sports centres of racing car circuits marked out with several shades of paint.

Laminate, the tough plastic material often used on kitchen counters, can be revitalised with paint. First wash it thoroughly with detergent solution and rinse, then sand with fine silicon carbide paper while the surface is still wet. Wash, rinse and allow to dry, then either apply two coats of alkyd gloss paint, sanding down with extra fine sandpaper and rinsing between coats, or apply one coat of enamel.

Melamine is a sprayed finish that resembles laminate but is less durable. Although it is seldom used anymore, homes from the forties and fifties may still have some lingering traces. If you aren't ready to replace it, you can paint it. Prepare the surface as for laminate, then paint with eggshell, gloss or enamel, or with emulsion topped by two coats of polyurethane varnish, depending on the degree of shine you require and the amount of wear the surface will receive.

Metal that's subject to stress from heat (as with radiators) or weather is best treated first with a metallic primer, which generally contains zinc chromate. This helps to resist corrosion and creates a barrier to protect the metal from moisture and

Grates and firebacks need two coats of a special heat-resistant paint.

the action of solvents in the paint. Metal may be painted with alkyd gloss paint but enamel gives a higher shine and a harder finish.

Radiators often look best if painted to match the wall, so the usual choice is gloss or eggshell finish. In practical terms, however, the most hard-wearing paint is radiator enamel which is heat-resistant and discolors less quickly than most conventional gloss paint. Prime the radiator with metal primer and apply radiator enamel while the heating is switched off. Then turn the boiler to maximum for two hours so that the enamel 'stoves' on for a hard finish. Radiator enamel may contain resins which make paint thinner an unsuitable solvent, so follow the manufacturer's instructions for cleaning brushes. As the color range is normally limited to white and magnolia, you may prefer to compromise

on durability and choose a gloss or semigloss paint to blend with the overall scheme.

Scoreboard green has a flat finish and is used for sign-boards and table tennis tables.

Tiles may be painted with special tile paint, or with enamel. Remove old paint from tiles with chemical stripper or – as heat may crack the surface – by sanding. Look for an enamel which resists heat to around 300°F if you are painting a fireplace surround or tiles behind a stove. Red tile paint is intended for quarry tiles and brickwork; a durable exterior grade is available for use on roofs and exterior masonry.

Fireplaces

Open fires are currently enjoying a revival, and the latest generation of imitation gas and log fires are convincing substitutes for the real thing. This means that the fireplace is once more an important feature in many rooms, a cosy place to gather on chilly winter nights. Even when not in use, it remains a focal point where plants and flowers can be displayed.

Top left: who could resist tea and toast by this nursery-style hearth? The supports and mantlepiece have been cissed crudely to suggest natural stone.

Top right: the lines and curves of this graceful fireplace are highlighted by the owner's choice of ornaments to stand on the mantlepiece.

Bottom, far left: a blocked-up fireplace needn't be an eyesore. Paint in white and use it as a 'vase' for colourful fabric flowers.

Bottom left: this classic Victorian fireplace has been lovingly restored, its black leading framing the contrasting decorative tiles.

Bottom right: a modern treatment for a traditional focal point – tongue and groove panels and quarry tiles make an eye-catching addition to a room.

Bottom, far right: a sumptuous marble fireplace lends this elegantly proportioned room an air of distinction and formal splendour.

Floors

The floor is often the bottom line for home decorators! Don't ignore its decorative potential which you can realize with a wide range of materials from cork and vinyl to ceramic or quarry tiles. Hard floorings like marble, slate and ceramic are expensive and luxurious but will last a lifetime; flexible materials like cork, rubber and vinyl are less durable but also less costly. Cheapest of all are the boards beneath your feet, which can be sanded and sealed, colour washed or stencilled, to suit your scheme.

Matt or gloss finish floors look equally effective in the appropriate settings. Degrees of sheen range from matt colour-rubbed boards to shiny ceramic tiles. Mimic their sheen with high gloss varnish applied to cork or wood for an easy-care shine.

This section concentrates on smooth floorings because they allow more scope for experimenting with design. Here we cover the basics of preparing the sub-floor, sanding and sealing floorboards and laying wood, tile and sheet floorings. That's just the beginning: to see the effects you can achieve by stencilling, spattering and combing, turn to the pages on advanced techniques. It could save you the cost of a new carpet. . .

Sub-floors

Whatever you choose to lay on top, the sub-floor must be free from damp, sound, clean and level.

Damp affects solid floors. Quarry tiles and flagstones were designed to cope with a degree of damp and if you have an old house where these have been laid you may be unaware of the problem. Test by taping a piece of plastic wrap to the floor and leave it for 48 hours. The edge of the film must be well sealed down. Any moisture that appears on the underside is formed by rising damp. Don't worry about any that collects on top – that's condensation. Although you should take steps to remedy this (by a better balance between heating and ventilation) it won't affect the floorcovering.

What can you do if you find damp? First call in a builder to establish the extent of the problem. If it's not severe or can't be completely cured (few old cottages, for example, are completely dry) you can keep damp at bay by sealing the sub-floor with diluted pva adhesive. You will need to remove the baseboard and take this protective coating up the wall to meet the level of the vapour barrier course. This is not the only method of coping with the problem; others include hot or cold tar, tarpaper, asphalt flooring adhesive and polyethylene sheeting – but none should be used as a substitute for expert advice!

If you're flooring over a suspended floor, ensure that the space is adequately ventilated or the floor may rot.

Structural defects occur if the joists supporting floorboards rot or move, causing the floor to sag. The odd loose joist can be fixed in place by packing the gap with slates and mortar for a tight fit, but if several are affected it's best to call in a specialist. You'll need to raise the boards to examine the joists. Lever them up with a wide 'bolster' chisel or spade and place a piece of wood underneath to stop the board from snapping back into place while you raise the rest of it. Stubborn floorboards, especially tongue and groove which slot tightly together, may have to be cut. Be careful not to cut into the joists, and use a floorboard saw or keyhole saw.

Clean the sub-floor thoroughly, using a commercial polish stripper if necessary or a solution of ½ gallon of cold water with half a cup of floor cleaning powder and one cup of ammonia. Scrub, rinse and allow the floor to dry. This is especially important before laying wood, tiles or sheet flooring because the adhesive may not stick to old polish or varnish. Rub old tiles or immovable flooring with steel wool to improve adhesion. You may need to prime wooden floors or board before laying ceramic tiles, if recommended by the adhesive manufacturer, or use diluted pva adhesive as a barrier coat.

Level sub-floors are essential as bumps and dips will be repeated rather than concealed by the new flooring and cause premature wear and tear. With floorboards the first step is to punch down nails and to countersink any screws which protrude – but be careful not to puncture any pipes or electric cables which lie beneath. (This process is particularly important if you intend to machine-sand the floor as an electric sander may catch on a nail.) If you find large gaps between floorboards,

it's best to cover them completely with hardboard, chipboard or plywood panels, depending on the weight of the floor they will bear.

Dips in concrete floors may be filled with a sand and mortar mix (1 part cement to 3 parts sand). Small quantities are best bought in a bag of dry mixed mortar available from home improvement stores. A little diluted pva adhesive applied to the area first will help bond the mortar to the surrounding area. Make a clean edge by tapping round the hole with a hammer and chisel (wear goggles to protect your eyes) and brush the crevice clean before filling it with the mortar. Apply with a filling knife or trowel and smooth it level. A crazed or sloping concrete floor should be treated with a screed or levelling compound.

Laying a sub-floor
First decide on the material you need to cover the boards.

Hardboard is cheapest. It is made from wood pulp pressed into thin sheets, approximately ¼ inch thick and 48 inches square. It provides a satisfactory sub-floor for carpet, cork or vinyl. (Ceramic tiles require a stronger base – use plywood.) Lay smooth side down so that the rough side helps the adhesive of the floorcovering laid over it to adhere. Condition the panels before use by sprinkling water on to the textured side and stacking them on edge for 48 hours in the room where they will be laid.

Chipboard consists of wood chips bonded to form a board and it's often used in place of floorboards in modern houses. Stouter tongue and groove chipboard can be used as a top-floor. Chipboard is thicker than hardboard and it must also be protected from damp.

Plywood looks most like wood. It's made from thin layers of wood stuck together so that the grain runs in opposite directions and comes in panels. It's the strongest material for a sub-floor and is strong enough to use as a top-floor: stain or seal it for an effective finish.

Make sure that no nails or screws protrude and that the floorboards are sound. Attach the panels to the floor at 1 foot intervals across, but 6 inches apart around the perimeter to hold the edge down firmly, using ring shank nails for chipboard and plywood, and hardboard nails for hardboard. To provide access for pipes, cut narrow strips to cover them. It's important to stagger the seams but don't bother to trim the panels to obtain a perfect fit unless you intend laying ceramic tiles which will need edge to edge support.

Attach the sub-floor firmly to make sure that it won't lift and remember to stagger the seams to avoid weak spots.

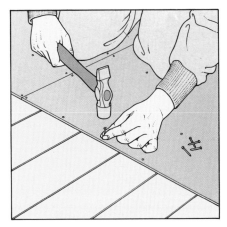

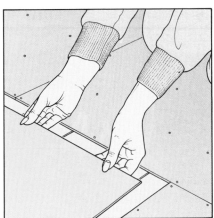

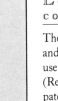

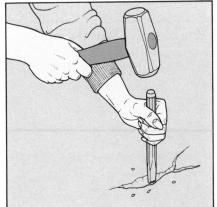

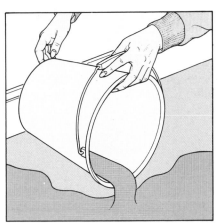

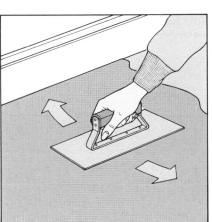

Levelling... concrete

The floor must be perfectly clean and free from grease before you use a self-levelling compound. (Remove any stubborn oily patches with paint thinner and steel wool.) Clean out cracks using a club hammer and chisel, taking care to avoid flying debris.

Now fill in the mortar, using a trowel, and smooth level. Mortar can be bought ready-mixed for small projects like this. Mix the compound to the consistency of thick cream and pour it onto the crack a little a time.

The floor must be perfectly clean and free from grease before you use a self-levelling compound. (Remove any stubborn oily patches with paint thinner and steel wool.) Mix the compound to the consistency of thick cream and pour it on to the floor a little at a time, spreading it around with a trowel. Make sure you work backwards, towards the door! The compound will take two to three hours to set.

Spread it around with a trowel or steel float as shown. Make sure you work backwards, towards the door! The compound will take two to three hours to set.

Treating existing wood floors

The boards beneath your feet are the one form of flooring that's yours for free. If you've decided on smooth flooring – particularly if you want a wooden floor – it makes sense to consider treating the existing floor before you buy an alternative. Not all floorboards repay the effort that's required, however, so take up the carpet and check the boards carefully before you start.

Are the boards hardwood (eg oak) or softwood (eg pine)?

Hardwood boards are almost always worth renovating, making a hard-wearing and attractive floor. If the floorboards are softwood you'll need to assess whether they are of suffi-cient quality to respond to sanding and sealing. If the boards are thin and splintering or worn and warped, it's better to cover them with new wood.

Are the boards patched or marked?

The odd cut or split plank is to be expected but a floor made up of different sizes and types of board won't look very attractive when exposed. If different varieties of wood have been used you may find it difficult to achieve a uniform col-our. This won't matter if you intend to paint the floor with an opaque colour or use a dark stain but may be important if you want a light or natural effect.

Have the boards been stained?

This isn't a problem if the entire floor has been treated but if only the perimeter is stained some difference in colour may remain after sanding. Test an area of stained floor by sanding it and then experimenting with wood stain and bleach until you are happy with the result. Then repeat the procedure on an unstained area and compare the results to decide whether you feel it is worth proceeding.

Are there gaps between the boards?

Any gaps should be packed with

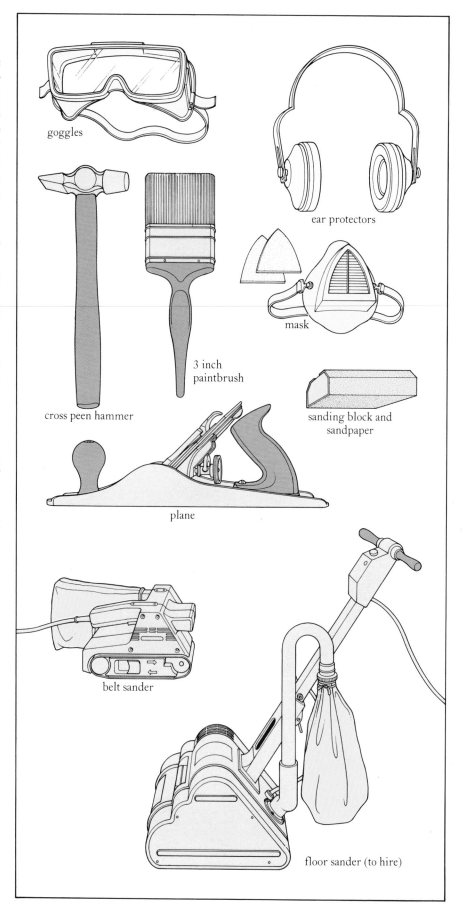

goggles

ear protectors

cross peen hammer

3 inch paintbrush

mask

sanding block and sandpaper

plane

belt sander

floor sander (to hire)

slivers of wood, wood filler or, if painting, papier-mâché. Cut wedge-shaped pieces of wood to match the boards, coat the sides with wood adhesive, tap into place with a hammer (protecting the sliver with a scrap of wood) and plane the surface level. Cracks and irregular gaps can be stopped with papier-mâché (made from crumpled newspaper soaked in diluted wallpaper paste) or wood filler. Remember that these materials will show through the seal so stain them to match the surrounding area or use suitably coloured filler. Gaps of more than ⅛ inch are difficult to fill. If the boards are widely spaced you can make the choice to lift and relay the floor (although this is worth doing only if the boards are of exceptional quality). Alternatively, cover the gappy boards with wood strip flooring – see page 88 – but remember that butt-jointed boards may shrink back and leave gaps.

Equipment

Ingrained dirt, polish, stain and paint are best removed by powered sanding equipment. If you are particularly lucky you may find that the boards are in such good condition that they respond to cleaning with steel wool and paint thinner and light hand-sanding along the grain.

If not, you will need to rent:
- a floor sander complete with disposal bag and abrasive.
- a belt sander (see page 60).
- protective equipment – goggles, dust mask and ear protectors.

You will also need:
- a nail punch or a blunt nail to recess nails before you start.
- a hammer.
- a plane for levelling the pieces of wood used for filling.
- a sanding block and abrasive paper for treating corners.
- a shavehook (see page 58).
- a 3 inch paintbrush for applying the sealer.

1

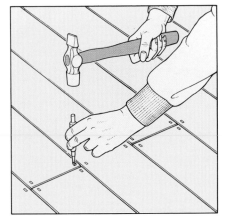

2

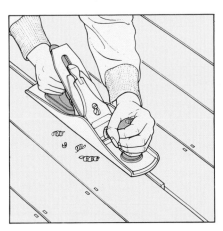

3

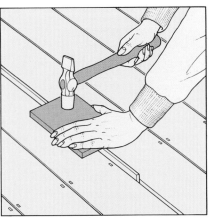

4

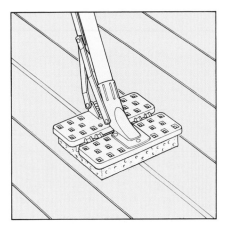

Preparation

Check that all the floorboards are sound and there is nothing protruding. Punch down nails and countersink screws to at least ⅛ inch beneath the surface, taking care not to puncture any pipes or cables.

Fill any gaps between the floorboards with wood slivers, wood filler or, if you intend painting, papier mâché. Apply wood adhesive to wedge-shaped pieces of wood and tap them into place with a hammer, protecting the slivers with a scrap.

Once the sliver is in place, plane it until it is level with the surrounding floorboards. You may need to stain the wood, wood filler or papier mâché to match the boards.

Thoroughly clean away all particles of dust, sawdust and shavings with a damp sponge. Use the minimum of water to avoid soaking the floorboards.

Sanding

Shut the windows and shut and tape up the door to prevent dust from seeping into the rest of the house.

Fit coarse abrasive to the power sander and work diagonally across the boards to remove the worst of the dirt, overlapping each sanded strip by about 3 inches. Keep the cable behind you at all times and hold the sander firmly. Don't allow the sander to settle on and dig into one spot. Vacuum the floor.

Now fit medium grade abrasive and sand up and down along the grain, overlapping as before. Switch off when you reach your starting point so that you don't sand the boards at right angles when you move on or you risk scratching them. Vacuum the floor.

Repeat using fine abrasive. Vacuum the floor again.

Go round the perimeter of the room with the belt sander, working along the grain.

Use a shavehook and sanding block to work into the corners and up to the baseboard.

Vacuum once more, then damp mop the floor to remove every trace of dust and allow to dry. Allow at least one day for power sanding and another to finish the work. Noise and vibration make this a tiring job, so you may prefer to spread the work over several days.

Sealing

It's important to make sure that the floor is completely free from dust before varnishing. You may prefer instead to wax polish the boards, but bear in mind that varnishing provides the most durable and easy-care surface. It isn't immune to wear – stiletto heels will puncture it and furniture will scratch it if dragged across the surface – and the floor will need to be resanded and revarnished every ten years or so.

First bleach or colour the floor if necessary. Use wood bleach to lighten the floor, wood stain to colour it.

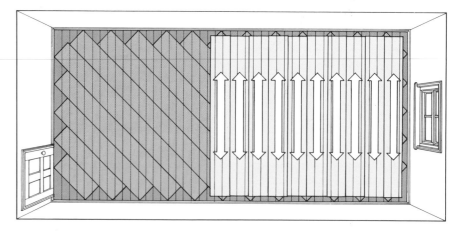

1. Begin by sanding diagonally with coarse abrasive to remove varnish and dirt.

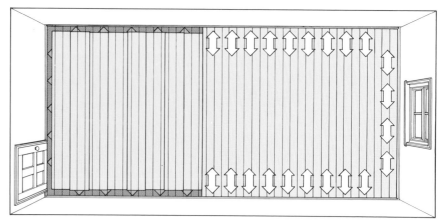

2. Next fit medium abrasive and sand along the grain, taking care to overlap.

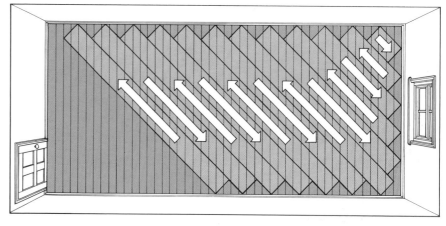

3. Use a belt sander to reach to the baseboard, sanding along the grain.

Apply wood stain along the grain with a soft cloth and remove the excess with a clean rag when dry. (You can use tinted varnish in place of a wood stain finish plus clear polyurethane, but it may be difficult to obtain an even colour and traffic areas will become noticeable as the colour wears away.)

Apply an initial coat of floor quality polyurethane varnish diluted with 10 percent paint thinner along the grain. Allow to dry out thoroughly and then sand lightly before the next coat. Apply two further coats of varnish.

Types of sealers

Cold cure varnish consists of two components which are mixed together to create a chemical bond which strengthens the finish. This is the toughest form of floor sealer, but its high gloss may make the wood look synthetic.

Floor sealer may contain alkyd resins which are not always as hard-wearing as polyurethane. It is particularly good for porous surfaces such as cork.

Polyurethane varnish is available in gloss, semigloss or matt finish. Not all types are recommended for use on floors, so check before you buy. Some brands should not be applied over existing varnish, so choose carefully if you want to renew a seal rather than start from scratch.

Tinted varnish is usually made in wood shades, but conventional colours are available too. These have a translucent effect which is modified by the natural colour of the wood but don't provide a total change of colour. Repeated applications will result in a deeper shade.

Wax polish is the traditional finish for floors. It brings out the richness of the wood but needs renewing – and removing – frequently, as a build-up of polish traps dirt and discolours the wood. It won't stand up to heavy use so it's better to choose polyurethane varnish for halls and living rooms – matt finish gives a similar effect. Wax polish is available as paste, which contains more wax, or in liquid form, which

Matt polyurethane varnish is just one of the ways of finishing sanded boards, providing a more durable surface than wax polish.

has a higher proportion of solvent to clean away the old layer as you apply the new one. (You will still need to strip the floor regularly, using paint thinner and steel wool.) Don't use the coloured polishes available for furniture on floors as the dye may be walked on to carpets.

Yacht varnish repels water but may not always have the resistance to abrasion that floors require. Check the product details before you buy.

Coverage and Drying Times

Product	Area covered per quart in square yards	Number of coats required on bare wood	Touch dry (in hours)	Recoatable (in hours)
cold cure varnish	12	3	3	16-24
floor sealer	12	2-3	1-3	16-24
polyurethane varnish	12-18	3-4	3	16-24
tinted varnish	18	1-2	3	16-24
		(apply on clear varnish)		
yacht varnish	12	3	3	24

Wooden Floors

Parquet, mosaic, strip or plank, polished, varnished, or covered in clear vinyl; softwood, hardwood or veneer – wood is the most versatile material used for floors. Whether the choice is to sand and polish the subfloor or to invest in parquet, wood forms a warm, hardwearing flooring which suits every style of decoration from modern minimalism to cosy, traditional rooms.

Far left, top: herringbone design has a timeless elegance which looks at home in a formal neo-classical room or in a casual contemporary setting.

Top left: wood strip floor is laid across this hallway to minimise its length. It is finished with several coats of polyurethane varnish to resist damp and dirt.

Below far left: sanded floorboards are divided into squares and intersected by black diamond shapes to simulate the appearance of marble tiles.

Below centre left: Trompe l'oeil 'carpet' runner in black and grey adds interest to this hall. Both 'carpet' and glossy black surround are varnished for protection.

Below centre right: boards stained black set the scene in this monochromatic sitting room, picking up the colour of the tables and window frames.

Below right: choose high gloss varnish to achieve this type of shine, or opt for moisture-resistant vinyl-coated boards, ideal for dining rooms and kitchens.

Wood

Wood is durable and attractive and, given a few coats of polyurethane varnish, relatively easy-care. There are three types generally available, mosaic flooring, wood strip and parquet.

All types are available finished or untreated. The finish varies from a vinyl seal to an acrylic coating. Untreated wood will need light sanding, then several coats of polyurethane varnish or wax polish. You should wait a few weeks for the floor to settle before sealing with polyurethane varnish, but (see page 82) weigh this against the amount of wear the floor is likely to receive. It's important to unwrap the flooring and allow it to condition in the room where it will be installed for a week before it is laid; you will also need to leave an expansion gap of about ½ inch around the perimeter of the room.

Laying a mosaic floor

Mosaic flooring is specifically designed for do-it-yourself use. It consists of solid or veneered wood panels about 18 inches square made up of small blocks arranged in a basketweave pattern on a backing. This is the easiest type of wood floor to lay because it's possible to separate the panels into squares or 'fingers' for working round obstacles.

First prepare the sub-floor. Lay hardboard over floorboards and make sure that a solid sub-floor is completely dry. You will also have to decide what to do about the expansion gap. The neatest – and most laborious – solution is to remove the baseboard and replace it when the floor is laid so that it covers the bare edge. Otherwise choose between an infill of flexible cork strip which will take up irregularities in the wall or quarter round moulding tacked on to the floor and stained and sealed to match.

1

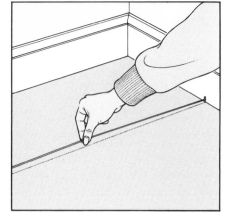

2

3

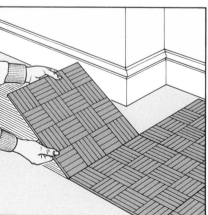

4

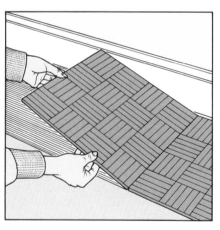

Laying a mosaic floor

Measure the wood panel and add ½ inch for expansion. Snap a chalked string this distance away from the longest uninterrupted wall. This will be your starting point. Lay whole panels over the floor as a trial run and adjust your starting point if you are left with awkward gaps at each end of the room (see tiling techniques, page 91).

Cut a stick or piece of cork strip to fill the expansion gap and use this and the chalk line as a guide. Apply adhesive to the floor (follow the manufacturer's recommendations when choosing the type) with a notched spreader, covering the area needed for one panel at a time.

Butt the panels up to each other but don't push them together as you will force adhesive on to the surface of the wood. Wipe away any excess adhesive immediately.

Lay whole panels first before you cut pieces to fill alcoves and doorways. Work up and down along the floor, checking each row as you go to make sure that it is straight.

When you need to cut a panel, place it over the last panel in the row. Place another on top so that its far edge is ½ inch away from the baseboard (allowing for the expansion gap). This will give you your cutting line.

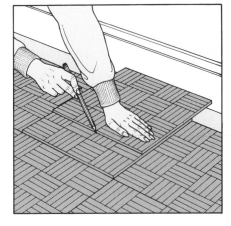

5

Cut the panel face upwards, using a tenon saw (see coving), spread adhesive on the back and put it carefully in place. Any excess adhesive should be wiped away before it starts to set.

6

If architrave protrudes, cut it away if possible and slide the panel underneath. Otherwise you will have to make a template and cut the pattern out with a jigsaw. Finish by attaching moulding to the baseboard with paneling nails (remember to mitre the corners) or fill the gap with cork edging strip.

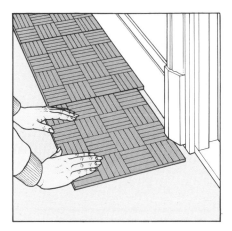

7

If the floor is unfinished, sand lightly, then vacuum the floor thoroughly and wipe with paint thinner to remove all dust. Seal the floor (see pages 82-3) with a primary coat of varnish diluted according to the manufacturer's directions (usually with 10 per cent paint thinner). Allow to dry, then sand lightly with 400 grit silicon carbide paper. Apply two further coats, sanding between applications.

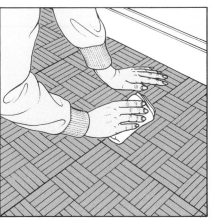

8

Ask the Professionals

Q How long will a polyurethane seal last?

A *You may need to 'refresh' the seal every two to three years by sanding lightly and adding another coat. After about ten years, however, areas of wear will become apparent and the seal will have worn thin. At this stage it's best to rent a power sander and remove all the varnish and a fine layer of wood and repeat the sealing process from the beginning.*

Q Can I use man-made board as a top-floor?

A *Yes, but only plywood or veneered chipboard will withstand heavy wear. Chipboard and hardboard will swell when damp so they should not be used in kitchens and bathrooms except as a sub-floor. You can colour and seal them for use in other rooms (though chipboard will soak up stain because it is so absorbent) but choose plywood if you want a strong and unusual living room or hall floor. If cut into evenly-sized panels and varnished with three coats of gloss finish polyurethane, it will look smart and resist wear.*

Q How do I sand unfinished mosaic flooring?

A *Because of its basketweave pattern, mosaic flooring has grain which runs in different directions. It's impractical to sand along it, so use an orbital sander and sand lightly at a 45° angle to minimise scratching. Take special care if you use a power sander on mosaic flooring that's already in place as the panels may be veneered with only a thin layer of hardwood. It's worth removing a section to see how much sanding the flooring will withstand before you start.*

Wood strip flooring

Wood strip looks like short, narrow planks which vary in thickness from 10 to 20 mm plus. It may be made of tongue and groove solid hardwood or veneered softwood, and is either laid to form a floating floor or 'secret nailed' with nails driven through the tongue and into the sub-floor at a 45° angle. Some wood strip flooring is designed to replace floorboards and is laid on top of the joists – worth considering if you have a timber sub-floor to replace.

Preparation of the sub-floor should be carried out in the same way as for mosaic flooring. It's best to lay a hardboard or plywood base over floorboards unless you are fitting a floor which is laid directly on to the joists. If you do want to lay wood strip on floorboards, it should run at right angles to them. Wood strip may also require an underlay – newspaper, polythene or one provided by the manufacturer. Methods of laying also vary, so follow the instructions provided with the product. General guidelines are given opposite.

You can also lay wood strip flooring in patterns if you prefer. Some types are available in a mixture of long and short lengths which may be mixed in the design of your choice or are intended to form a 'Dutch' design where short pieces are laid at right angles to long. It's also possible to lay some varieties of wood strip in a herringbone pattern. Whichever you choose, remove doors before you start as these will need to be trimmed to fit when the floor is laid.

Parquet floors are made from individual wood blocks. These may be tongue and groove and laid to form a 'floating' floor or stuck down, in the traditional herringbone or 'brick bond' pattern. Parquet flooring is expensive and limited in availability. It demands a flat sub-floor and is best laid professionally.

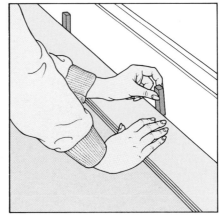

1

2

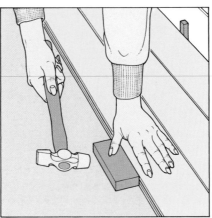

3

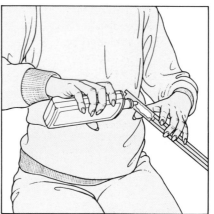

4

Laying wood strip flooring

Snap a string covered in chalk next to the longest, or easiest, wall to mark a staight line. (If the room is particularly narrow you may prefer the strips to run across the room to give an illusion of width, though this will entail more cutting.) Use a batten or offcut of wood to fix the 12 mm expansion gap.

If the flooring has fixing clips, hammer into adjacent lengths 750 mm apart, making sure that they are staggered. If adhesive is recommended, glue the tongues and grooves. If 'secret nailing', fix the first row to the floor with pins 250 mm apart, groove to the wall. Drive pins close to the main plank at a 45° angle through the tongue into the floor.

Push the groove of the next piece over the tongue, tapping with a hammer on to a protective offcut of wood and repeat.

Complete the flooring in the method you have chosen, clipping and glueing or nailing and making sure that any joins are staggered to avoid weakness.

Glue end pieces if using the clip or adhesive method; butt join the ends if you are fixing the floor by secret nailing. Sand lightly with a finishing sander, working along the grain, and seal (see pages 82-3).

Tiles and Tiling

More flooring is available in tile form than in any other. You can choose from ceramic, quarry (unglazed clay) and marble for a hard, long-lasting floor, carpet or sealed and unsealed cork for warmth or rubber, thermoplastic and vinyl for economy and resilience. For a traditional country kitchen, you could fit a flagstone floor, and for a living or dining room make timber tiles from plywood, stained and sealed for a natural or multi-coloured effect.

Tiles are easier to handle than bulky rolls of sheet flooring and there's less waste in narrow halls, rooms with awkward alcoves and bathrooms cluttered with obstacles like a pedestal basin or wc. Remember that laying tiles over a large area is a laborious business – and that there's a world of difference between cutting and laying ceramic tiles and the self-adhesive vinyl sort.

Ceramic floor tiles are made from clay which is glazed to provide an impermeable surface. They are thicker, larger and less glossy than those used on walls and available in an almost endless variety of colours and styles to suit modern and traditional settings. Oblong (average size 10 by 20 cm, 4 by 8 inches) and square (usually 20 cm, 8 inches square) shapes are the most popular but you can buy hexagonal and Provençal designs too, though these are more difficult to lay. Ceramic tiles are extremely hard-wearing but correspondingly expensive. They are also cold and can be hard on the feet. It's important to pick the right type of tile for the area of use – frostproof for steps and patios, slip-resistant for kitchens, for example – and to choose the correct adhesive. You'll need a waterproof adhesive for shower cubicles and bathroom floors, a frostproof one for outdoor use and a heatproof variety when tiling round a fireplace.
*Ease of laying: **

Cork creates a warm and attractive floor but as it is porous it must be treated before use. Unsealed cork is relatively inexpensive but needs at least three coats of polyurethane varnish or floor seal to withstand wear. (Cork tiles may be waxed for use in bedrooms or areas of light wear if you prefer, but this offers little resistance to damp.) In kitchens, bathrooms and halls it's worth laying sealed cork tiles which have been dipped in vinyl so that even the edges and backs are protected against moisture penetration. These are often triple the price of natural cork tiles; a cheaper version with a sealed surface should be sufficient for playrooms, dining and living rooms. Cork tiles are usually 30 cm, 12 inches square and are available in white or partly coloured finishes (red, green and black are the most popular) as well as natural shades. You'll need a special cork adhesive for laying the tiles and it's advisable to fit hardboard over floorboards as any movement of the sub-floor will cause the tiles to crack.
*Ease of laying: ***

Lino tiles are back in favour, now for smart interiors rather than as a substitute for carpet. Linoleum is quite different from vinyl which it superficially resembles. It's made from a blend of natural products, notably linseed oil, cork and resin, rather than plastic, and modern lino is thick enough to resist the hardest wear. Colours are often more subtle than those of vinyl, and it has a more delicate sheen than vinyl but the 'new' lino may not be cheap; expect to pay as much for top quality lino as for ceramic tiles. Lino should be polished or treated with a compatible seal (oleo-resinous rather than polyurethane) and although it is durable it may crack if laid directly over floorboards and will deteriorate when damp, so take care not to over wet when cleaning.
*Ease of laying: ***

Quarry tiles are made from unglazed ceramic. They're often smaller than ceramic tiles (15 cm, 6 inches square, though Provençal and hexagonal shapes are also available) and restricted in colour to earth shades like terracotta, brown and black. Quarry tiles make a classic flooring that looks attractive in any setting, modern or traditional. They are very hard-wearing and surprisingly easy-care; finish with linseed oil and turpentine, floor seal or polish if you demand a shine or simply sweep, mop and scrub when necessary. They are often laid on a bed of mortar which is more difficult to manipulate than tile adhesive and their thickness is tricky to cut. Not recommended for beginners.
*Ease of laying: **

Rubber is an industrial flooring which has been adopted for use in the home. Its profiled (often studded) design is slip-resistant and suits contemporary interiors but can be difficult to clean as the texture traps dirt. Rubber can be natural, synthetic (latex), or a mixture of the two. It is strong, waterproof and more flexible, but also more expensive, than most vinyl.
*Ease of laying: ***

Vinyl is the most popular material for tiles. The range varies from cheap thermoplastic tiles with vinyl added to improve wear, to self-adhesive tiles, vinyl-sealed cork and top quality tiles which contain 70 per cent vinyl or more and cost as much as many ceramics. There's a tendency for vinyl to copy other materials, such as brick, ceramic or wood, and even 'plain' vinyl tiles often have a flecked finish to disguise imperfections; you pay more for perfectly plain colours which demand a high standard of manufacture. Many ranges are designed for diy installation but if you want to lay an elaborate pattern or an expensive brand, employ a specialist flooring contractor.
*Ease of laying: ****

Equipment

For laying ceramic and quarry tiles you will need:
- chalked string.
- sticks for marking the area.
- a set square to check right angles.
- a wide-bladed scraper or a trowel.
- a spirit level.
- a notched spreader.
- a wheeled tile cutter with jaws to cope with thick floor tiles (or rent a specialist floor tile cutter).
- pincers for snipping tiles.
- a tile file to smooth the edges.
- suitable adhesive or mortar.
- grout for floor tiles.
- two sponges.

For laying cork, rubber and vinyl tiles you will need:
- chalked string.
- a notched spreader.
- a trimming knife.
- sharp scissors.

For cutting plywood or chipboard tiles you will need to rent:
- a circular saw fitted with a masonry cutting blade.

Adhesives

Always be guided by the tile manufacturer's instructions as products vary in their requirements. The following is a general guide.

For ceramic and quarry tiles use
- a waterproof ceramic tile adhesive for showers and bathrooms.
- a frostproof tile adhesive for steps and balconies, depending on the climate.
- a heat-resistant tile adhesive for fireplaces and stoves.
- a conventional ceramic tile adhesive or mortar for solid floors.
- a flexible tile adhesive for suspended floors.

For cork tiles . . . choose special cork tile adhesive.

For rubber and vinyl tiles . . . choose acrylic floor tile adhesive.

You'll need to apply a thin bed (⅛ inch thick) of adhesive for tiles with a smooth back, a thick bed (¼

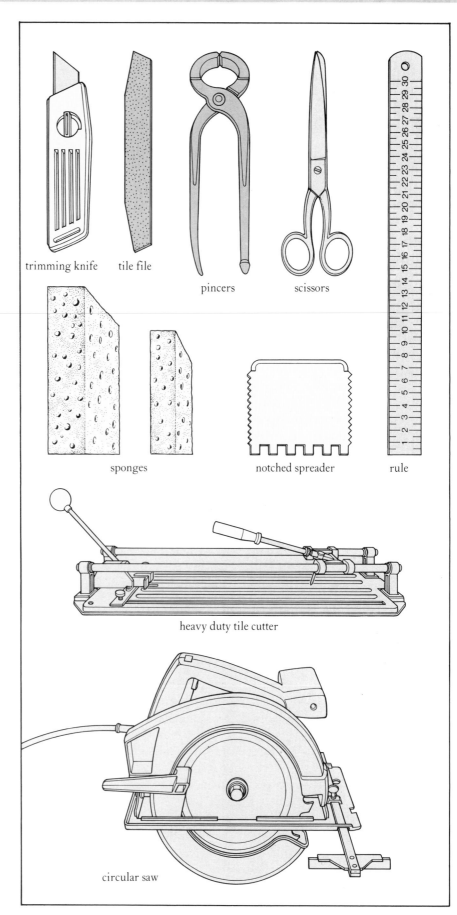

trimming knife   tile file

pincers   scissors

sponges   notched spreader   rule

heavy duty tile cutter

circular saw

inch thick) for studded tiles or irregular floors (though if the sub-floor is very uneven you should lay a self-levelling compound before you begin) and mortar (made from 1 part cement to 3 parts of sand) for extra-thick quarry tiles.

Prepare the sub-floor (see pages 78-9). Lay plywood over floorboards and prime it with diluted pva adhesive (or a primer recommended by the manufacturer) to form a sealing coat. Fill any patches in concrete or use self-levelling compound if it is uneven (see page 79) and allow screed a fortnight to dry before tiling. (New concrete should be left for one month.) It's possible to tile over existing tiles, quarry or ceramic, as long as these are sound and firmly attached to the sub-floor but don't try to tile over vinyl.

Laying ceramic and quarry tiles

Find your starting point. The centre is the best place when tiling a square room so that any cut tiles fall at the edges where they will be less noticeable. (In an irregular room or hall, it's better to start laying tiles by the longest uninterrupted wall – see overleaf.) You'll need the chalked string to mark the middle (by snapping it twice across the room from opposite walls; ignore alcoves and chimney breasts).

Now lay a dry run. It's important to keep the number of tiles you'll have to cut to an absolute minimum because ceramic floor tiles, especially quarries, can be brutes to cut. Aim to finish with half tiles on either side – wide gaps look strange and narrow ones are awkward to fill – and adjust your starting point to suit. Remember that cut tiles will look as prominent in front of a fireplace as they would in the centre of the room so plan carefully.

Lay the second tile above the first and the third to its right. Subsequent rows are laid diagonally, facing the corner of the room.

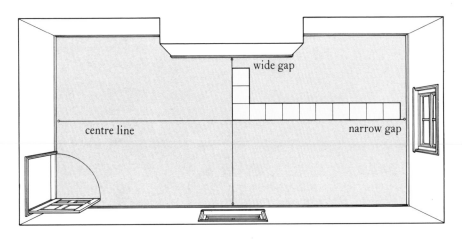

1. Find the centre of the room by snapping two lengths of chalked string across. This is the best place to start when tiling most rooms, but if you are tiling a narrow or irregular room, such as a hall, start by the nearest uninterrupted wall. Lay a dry run of tiles to minimise cutting and avoid wastage.

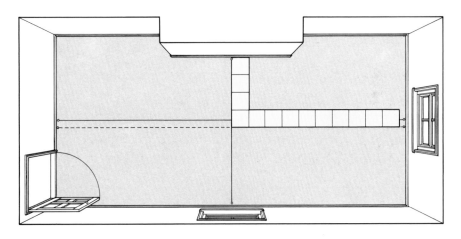

2. If you are left with a wide gap (more than half a tile wide) at the end of a row, adjust the starting point by moving it to accommodate another tile. If however the resulting gap is less than 3 inches wide it's better to leave the starting point at the centre of the room and accept the wastage, as narrow perimeter tiles can be awkward to cut and look obtrusive.

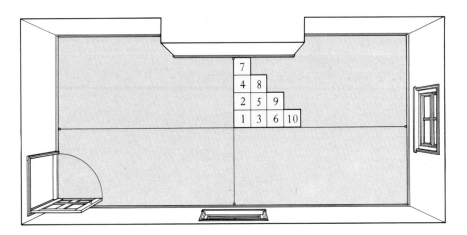

3. Treat each quarter of the room in turn, ending with that nearest the door. Lay the tiles in the order shown here, fanning outwards from the starting point and working towards the baseboards and fireplaces.

Ask the Professionals

Q Can I lay ceramic tiles upstairs?

A *Yes, provided you lay ply-wood over the floorboards and use a flexible ceramic floor tile adhesive to cope with any movement. If you lay ceramic tiles directly on to floorboards they will crack. If you want to tile a larger area check to establish whether your floorboards can support the load.*

Q How durable is vinyl?

A *Vinyl tiles vary in quality. They may contain from as little as 25 per cent vinyl to 75 per cent or more. Like most synthetics vinyl dyes more brilliantly than natural materials and is waterproof. Depending on your decor, vinyl can be used all over the house.*

Q Should I choose quarry or ceramic tiles for my kitchen?

A *The main differences are in appearance and price. They require similar installation techniques and wear equally well, though as quarries are unglazed the surface may become pitted. Quarries may be half the price of ceramic tiles and have a casual, country appeal. There are often natural variations in colour in a batch. Ceramic tiles are more formal and are available in patterns as well as plain colours. The glaze gives them a slightly colder look, but in a kitchen choose a textured, non-slip style with less shine.*

1

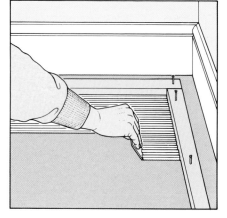

2

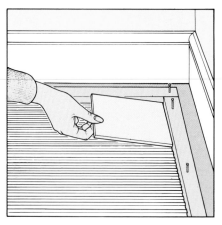

3

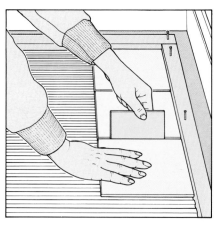

4

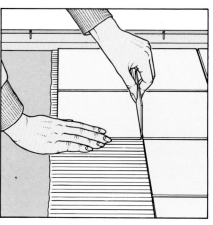

Laying ceramic and quarry tiles

Mark the limit of whole tiles with wooden sticks and check the right angles with a set square.

Spread adhesive over the floor with the notched spreader to cover a square yard.

Lay the tiles according to your dry run (see page 91). Work towards the door so that you don't have to step on the newly-laid tiles and dislodge them or embed them too deeply.

Use a piece of stiff cardboard or individual spacers to maintain an even grouting gap (remove them as you go) and check each row with a spirit level to ensure that the tiles are the same height. If there's any disparity, take them up and reset, using more or less adhesive as required.

Lay the second row of tiles using cardboard or spacers to ensure an even gap between it and the first. Leave the tiled floor for 24 hours before installing cut tiles or grouting. If you have to walk over the floor during this time, lay a 'crawl board' of plywood on top to spread the load. Then remove your marker sticks.

Cutting and grouting

To cut an edge tile, place it over the last whole tile in the row, covering it exactly. Put a spare tile on top of these two and push it firmly against the wall to cover the gap. Where this tile crosses the second tile, draw a line.

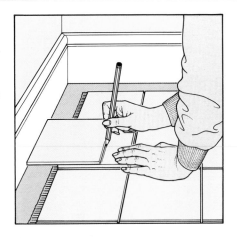

Use a cutter that has a wheel to score the tiles and jaws to hold them for cutting, or rent a floor tile cutter (especially useful for quarry tiles).

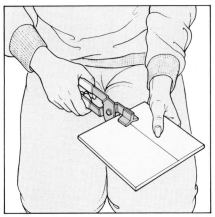

To fit the tile around obstacles such as pipes and alcoves, mark a line or pattern on the tile. (You may need to make a template.) Nibble away with pincers; particularly stubborn tiles may need help from a hammer and chisel. (Wear goggles to protect your eyes if you resort to this.)

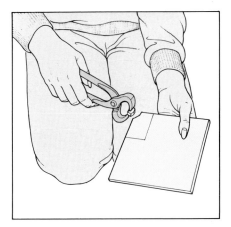

When the shape has been nibbled away, smooth the cut edge with a tile file, spread adhesive on the back and fix in place.

Apply grout a square yard at a time with a dry sponge and level it off with a rounded popsicle stick. (Wear rubber gloves to protect your skin from irritation.) Wipe off the excess with the damp sponge. When it has set, polish with a clean, dry sponge or cloth.

Ask the Professionals

Q Which tiles are the easiest to clean?

A *Ceramic tiles need the least attention, though because the glaze makes them slippery you must wipe all spills immediately. Damp mop them regularly using a solution of dishwashing liquid and warm water (don't add too much detergent or it will smear). For a satisfying shine, rinse and rub over with a dry cloth. Unsealed quarry tiles are even easier because you can omit the polishing process. However, if you want to produce a shine you'll have to seal them periodically with linseed oil and turpentine and finish with wax polish. Vinyl and vinyl-sealed cork are simple to care for, provided you avoid harsh abrasive powders which are difficult to dissolve and may scratch the clear vinyl surface. Top with an emulsion polish if you like (never wax) but remember that repeated applications will build up and should be removed with ammonia and cleaning powder (see page 78) at regular intervals; it's better to concentrate on regular cleaning using the smallest amount of detergent necessary to remove grease. Rubber is also easy-care but profiled designs are difficult to clean — the same goes for heavily textured vinyl tiles, though you may not notice until you move the stove! Take particular care not to over wet polyurethane-sealed cork and wood as the base materials will deteriorate when damp.*

Brick floor tiles should be swept and cleaned with mild detergent and warm water solution and rinsed. Clay bricks should then be dried. Marble tiles should be cleaned with care.

Tiled Floors

Tiles make a virtue of convenience. Some materials have always been cut into tiles to make them easier to handle — marble and stone, which are heavy to transport, and ceramic and quarry tiles, which need to be fired in a kiln. Vinyl and cork tiles are particularly easy to lay and so popular that many sheet floorings are designed to simulate the appearance of a tiled floor.

Top left: vinyl tiles substitute for marble in this dramatic black and white hall. The flecks not only simulate veining but conceal marks made in manufacture.

Top right: the real thing. Marble has a unique lustre and combines resistance to wear with a natural shine. Tiles made from a veneer of marble reduce the cost.

Below far left: stone and slate should not be concealed by carpets. Though a traditional form of flooring they are equally suited to modern interiors.

Below centre left: carpet in the kitchen becomes a practical proposition with this trompe l'oeil 'rug' set in a surround of plain ceramic tiles.

Below centre right: white tiles provide an uncluttered and unusual background to an otherwise feminine and frilly bedroom.

Below near right: ceramic floor tiles are available in a range of shapes and sizes. Here companion tiles form a border which defines the shape of the hall.

Laying cork, rubber and vinyl tiles

Prepare the sub-floor as for ceramic and quarry tiles and prime board if the manufacturer recommends this. For a sub-floor laid over floorboards, hardboard or chipboard can be substituted for plywood.

Find your starting point using chalked string, lay a dry run of tiles and adjust the starting point if necessary. Cork and vinyl are easy to cut, but as they are large, cut tiles are more obvious. Minimise the number you'll need to divide.

Lay tiles following the order on p.91, if starting from the centre of the room, on p.92 if tiling along the longest uninterrupted wall. Spread a yard of adhesive at a time if it is necessary. Peel the backing from the corner of self-adhesive cork and vinyl tiles and try to position them correctly the first time as adjustment may weaken the bond.

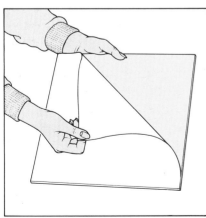

Cork tiles have a natural warmth and resilience. Choose pre-sealed tiles or coat with polyurethane for maximum resistance to wear.

Cut edge tiles with scissors or a trimming knife (best for complex patterns) using a spare tile as a template. Lay the tile to be cut to cover the last whole tile. Put the spare tile on top to cover the gap and draw a line where it crosses the tile. This shows you where to cut the tile to fit the gap. Mark a pattern on cardboard to copy the outline of architrave, trace it on to the tile and cut with a trimming knife.

Sand unsealed cork lightly using an orbital sander, vacuum thoroughly and wipe with paint thinner. Then apply three coats of polyurethane varnish (the first coat should be diluted with 10 per cent paint thinner) or floor sealer.

Left: prepare the sub-floor (above) and lay cork tiles as shown on pages 91-92. Remember to remove the backing from self-adhesive tiles first (left).

Right: mark and cut the board or plywood into panels first (above). After laying, sand lightly and apply stain, if used, and varnish (below) for protection.

Laying chipboard or plywood tiles

If the sub-floor is particularly uneven, cover it with hardboard (on a wooden floor) or self-levelling compound (on a solid floor).

Cut the panels, previously marked to the required size, with a circular saw.

Decide on your starting point, marking the centre of the room or an angle by the longest wall opposite the door with chalked string. Leave a 3/8 – 1/2 inch expansion gap.

Spread pva adhesive on the floor to cover the area taken by one panel. Lay whole panels first, then tackle the edges. (See the technique for laying mosaic floors on page 87.)

Allow the adhesive to set for 24 hours, then sand lightly with a finishing sander and apply wood stain if required, then three coats of polyurethane varnish, sanding lightly between each one.

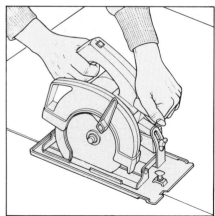

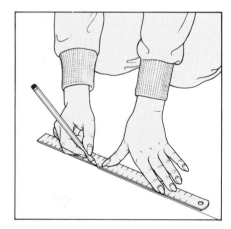

Sheet flooring

Sheet flooring today means vinyl. Although rubber is available in wide widths, it is generally designed for contract use – in offices, for instance – and it is difficult for the do-it-yourself customer to acquire.

There are several types of vinyl, all based on the sandwich principle. The thicker the sandwich, the more resilient – and expensive – the flooring.

Sheet vinyl consists of a clear vinyl wear layer which protects the printed pattern and backing beneath.

Cushioned vinyl has the same wear layer and print, with an aerated foam layer (the 'cushion') over the backing which can be made of mineral felt or reinforced with fiberglass. Fiberglass backed types are often called 'lay flat' vinyls. They can be folded for transport home and need securing only at doors and beneath heavy appliances, like the washing machine and refrigerator which need to be moved from time to time.

Extra-thick cushioned vinyl adds foam backing for the ultimate in warmth and resilience.

Most vinyls are available in six-, nine- or twelve-foot widths to eliminate seams, though you'll still have to join widths to fill alcoves if you want to avoid wastage.

When should you choose sheet flooring rather than tiles?

Tiles are easier to fit round obstacles. Choose them for small, awkwardly shaped rooms, such as bathrooms and lobbies, and very large rooms with numerous alcoves and fireplaces or with walls which are out of true, where sheet flooring may be difficult to manipulate.

Sheet flooring is recommended for large, regular rooms where there are few obstructions. Choose sheet vinyl for a kitchen, hall (buy a twelve-foot width with a regular or random design here and lay it sideways to

Sheet vinyl flooring is stylish and practical in a busy hallway.

reduce the number of seams), or playroom. It's quite feasible to fit sheet flooring in a small area where there's only one obstruction, but imagine trying to lay it in a bathroom where you may have to contend with a pedestal basin, bidet, toilet and bath! If you hanker after the luxury of cushioned vinyl here, choose cushioned vinyl tiles. Don't buy sheet flooring for this type of situation (unless you are both skilled and confident). Remember that although you can cover a large area more quickly with sheet flooring than with tiles, large rolls can be hard to handle on your own.

Preparing the sub-floor

Although you can lay sheet vinyl directly over floorboards, it's a false economy and eventually lines will appear as the vinyl moulds itself to the boards. So lay hardboard on a wooden sub-floor and screed an uneven concrete one as shown on page 79, making sure to check for damp and filling any holes in the concrete with an acrylic filler. You can lay vinyl flooring over sound ceramic, quarry, or solid vinyl tiles, but you should remove textured vinyl tiles and existing vinyl sheet. This may be quite a job; try stripping away the top layer and soaking the backing in the ammonia, detergent and water stripping solution mentioned on page 78. It should then be possible to lift it off with a paint scraper but however difficult this may prove, don't be tempted to sand it as you may release harmful asbestos fibres into the atmosphere. You can lay vinyl flooring over thermoplastic tiles if you cover them first with unwaxed brown paper. Use a similar barrier if you don't know what material has been used for the sub-floor and it can't be removed.

Measuring up

Measure the room at its longest and widest points, halfway into door openings so that the vinyl won't fall short at entrances. Add 20 inches to each measurement to allow for trimming and shrinkage – not all vinyls are stable. This will give you some idea of the width of flooring you require. Sometimes you will have a choice – if the area of the room is 10 × 12 feet for instance. If there are alcoves it may be cheaper to go for extra length rather than a wider width; it would be uneconomical, for example, to order a 12 foot width for a room that's nine feet square except for two 30-inch-deep recesses. Remember to allow for pattern matching (if applicable) and ensure that you have sufficient flooring left over for any future repairs.

When the flooring is delivered, take it into the room where it will be laid, unwrap and unroll it. Then roll it up in the opposite direction, pattern outwards, lay it on its side and leave it to acclimatise for 48 hours. Don't stand it on edge as the weight may cause cracking.

Equipment

You will need:
- a steel ruler.
- a trimming knife.
- large scissors.
- a paint scraper for pushing the vinyl into corners.
- a soft broom for ironing out bumps.
- a 'scribing block' made from a scrap of wood for transferring the shape of obstacles on to paper.
- thick paper for cutting templates.
- a pencil.
- acrylic flooring adhesive and/or double-sided tape or binder bars (according to the manufacturer's instructions) to hold the flooring firm at doorways.
- a notched spreader.
- a seam roller if necessary.

1

2

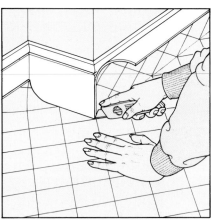

3

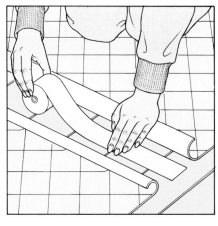

4

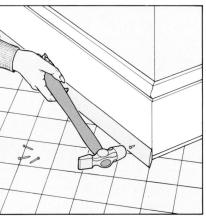

Neatening up

Snip a series of release cuts so that the vinyl no longer buckles at the corners. Push the vinyl into internal corners and cut away a small triangle, trimming a little at a time.

Cut diagonal slits at doorways and external corners, pressing well into the corner before you cut, so that the vinyl lies flat. Press out any bulges with the broom.

Lay-flat flooring can often be secured with double-sided tape. Use this to join widths, as shown, at doorways and beneath heavy appliances like the range and washing machine.

Cut the vinyl too short? Tack quarter-round moulding to the baseboard to conceal the gap. This remedial action also helps if the vinyl has shrunk or the floor is very uneven.

Laying techniques

Lay the roll diagonally across the room. Unroll it gradually, moving it into position as you go. Lay it flat on the floor with a minimum 2 inch overlap all round and smooth into place with the broom. If the walls are out of true, adjust the flooring so that it looks straight to the eye. Make pencil marks on the baseboard as a guide.

If the flooring you have chosen is subject to shrinkage, trim roughly with scissors to give an 8 inch overlap on all sides and leave for two weeks. When you are ready to trim push the vinyl hard against the baseboard with a scribing block or paint scraper. Place the blade of the trimming knife in the angle between baseboard and floor and cut carefully, keeping blade upright.

If you need to join widths, overlap the two sheets. Match the pattern, working from the centre outwards, and cut through the double thickness holding the trimming knife against a straight edge. Don't try this with extra-thick foam-backed vinyls. For these, you will need to cut a straight edge along the first sheet, place it over the second and cut through it for a perfect match. Now apply the adhesive. Check with the manufacturer's instructions; some vinyl may need to be stuck down all over, others it's only necessary to secure at the edges and seams. If this is the case apply a 6 inch deep band of adhesive at the beginning and end of each sheet, across the doorway and under any heavy appliances which are likely to be moved. Press the vinyl into position immediately and wipe away any excess which may damage the face of the flooring. Lay-flat flooring may not require any adhesive at all, though it's still advisable to secure it with tape or adhesive under washing machines and so on. Secure it at the doorway with double-sided tape or a binder bar, as the manufacturer suggests.

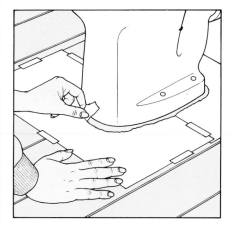

1

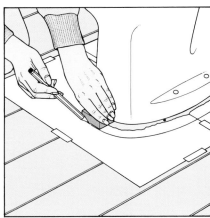

2

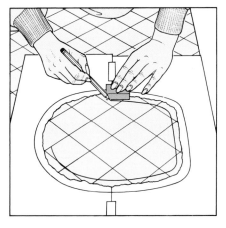

3

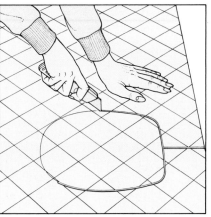

4

Cutting round obstacles

This is where your scribing block comes in. Place a piece of thick paper to overlap half the base of the toilet or other obstacle. Cut roughly round it so that you have half the basic shape, then repeat on the other side.

Press the scribing block against the base of the obstacle and push it slowly round, tracing its outline on to the paper with a pencil. This faithfully transfers the shape of the obstacle.

Lay the paper pattern over the flooring and trace another line with the scribing block on to the flooring, this time following the line on your template and holding the pencil against the other side of the scribing block.

Cut the flooring along this line with a trimming knife and make a cut at the back to allow for access. Then secure in place.

Hard floorings

Marble, slate, stone – if you de-mand the best then there's nothing like the real thing, but be warned – luxurious as they are, such hard floorings are cold, costly and diffi-cult to lay. Cheaper hard floors include brick and concrete, common or – literally – garden materials you might not want in the sitting room but which can look effective in basements and conservatories. Be-cause of their weight, all these floorings should be restricted to the ground floor and you should include a vapour barrier, such as thick polyethylene sheet, before installa-tion to prevent rising damp. With the exception of concrete all the following floorings look best in their natural state, and may be spoiled if sealed or polished.

Stone and brick are an integral part of a house, adapting to changing lifestyles.

Brick

Ordinary bricks won't do – you need SW (severe weathering) quality clay or calcium silicate. Bricks vary in thickness from paving bricks 1 inch deep to the regular 2½ inch size, or you can cheat by choosing thin brick floor tiles. Most clay bricks are red, but gold, gray and brown are also available. Calcium silicate bricks are much lighter, ranging from white to beige, and it's also possible to buy engineering bricks, which are denser and less absorbent than clay. Make sure new concrete is completely dry before laying bricks. The bricks should then be set in a screed of bricklaying mortar (calcium silicate bricks require a special mix) in one of the traditional basketweave, brick bond, or herringbone patterns. Cut when necessary with a wide bolster chisel and club hammer – not a job for the average do-it-yourself practitioner. Brick floors should be swept and cleaned with mild detergent and warm water solution and rinsed. Clay bricks should then be dried as they absorb water.

Concrete

The ugly sister of hard floorings can look quite respectable given a coat of flooring paint or set in small slabs. Pre-cast concrete slabs are sold at builders' merchants and garden centers. The most popular size is 18 inches square but the smaller 9 inch size looks better indoors. Brick-shape concrete blocks are available but, as they need to be bedded in with a plate vibrator, they are not suitable for home installation. The same applies to concrete paving which will have to be cut to fit. Both slabs and blocks are available in coloured finishes: pink, yellow and brilliant white, as well as the usual grey. 'One piece' concrete floors are made from a mix of sand, Portland cement and aggregate either mixed on the spot or delivered ready-mixed – in which case you must be waiting when it arrives. It is poured into an area defined by the 'form', a barrier of planks which holds the concrete in place, and is smoothed level with a wooden tamping beam. Allow a week to ten days for the floor to dry. Concrete can be scrubbed with powder floor cleaner dissolved in warm water and an occasional mild bleach solution.

Marble

Marble is expensive, but you might want to set a small piece in mortar to serve as a hearth-stone or step. Marble is a form of limestone with a gloss and veined appearance. It is so expensive that it is now often found in tile form with a thin layer used as a veneer and backed by other materials. Marble is very hard-wearing but it's liable to stain. Clean by damp-mopping and bleach stains with lemon juice, hydrogen peroxide or commercial cleaner.

Slate

Like marble, slate is another expensive material usually reserved for small areas such as hearths. Its colour range is restricted to grey-greens and blues and it has a textured surface. Sweep and then wash slate (it's naturally moisture-resistant) with a mild detergent solution applied with a brush to clean out the crevices. Treat with a mixture of equal parts linseed oil and paint thinner for a sheen.

Stone

Natural stone varies in colour from cream to grey. Flagstones are a traditional form of flooring made from local materials which were once cheap and readily available. Neither is true today, so consider buying reconstituted stone. Stone should be set in mortar, and although very durable it is porous and will mark. Sweep and damp mop regularly and treat stains carefully, as for marble.

Ask the Professionals

Q What bricks should I buy for the floor of my country kitchen? I want a traditional red-brick herringbone effect.

A *You need 'paviors', clay bricks suitable for flooring use. Ordinary wall bricks may not be strong enough, and in some cases the colour does not go all the way through, making chips and scratches especially noticeable. Some facing bricks will be suitable and you won't need the frost-resistant MW bricks for interior use. For expert advice consult a brick factory or dealer. Avoid calcium silicate or engineering bricks; although perfectly durable they won't give the rustic effect that you obviously have in mind.*

Q Marble flooring would suit the formal style of the hall in my nineteenth-century house but I can't afford the amount required. Is there any alternative which would convey the same style?

A *Think about marble tiles which cut the cost by reducing the marble used to a thin surface layer, or choose a vinyl tile substitute. A variety of marble and terrazzo (marble chip) effects are available in classic colours, based on traditional flooring patterns. In addition, vinyl is warm and resilient and easier to keep clean than the natural materials it simulates. It won't last quite as long, but it should certainly suit all domestic requirements. Alternatively, cut plywood tiles as described on page 97 and 'marble' them using the technique shown on page 158, for a cheap but realistic effect.*

Special Finishes

Discover the variety of finishes you can achieve with paint, paper, and a little know-how. This section introduces you to the effects you can produce with borders and with patterned paint, not yet available straight from the can but simple to achieve with a sponge, a bunch of rags, or even a scrubbing brush. Use it to sponge, rag or stipple walls for a misty finish, to dignify (or disguise) junk furniture with a realistic marble or tortoiseshell effect or to create a colourful mural. If you are confident of your artistic ability, try freehand painting on fabric; if not, try stencilling for a fool-proof effect or have fun spattering fireplaces and floors.

A sponged, textured finish creates a soft, creamy background to focus the attention on the painting.

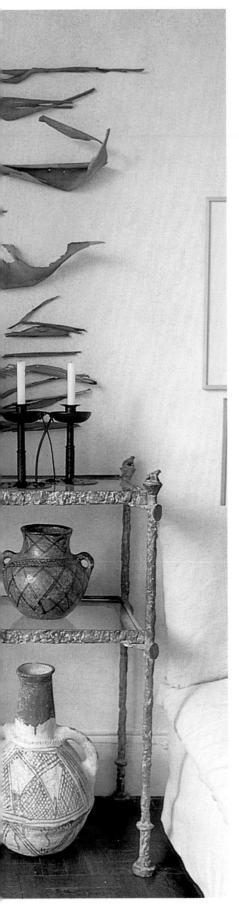

*Left: walls and woodwork sponged in grey over cream combine the
colours of console table, urns and ornaments to enhance their effect.
Top: azure blue and lime yellow applied to a neutral
background give a clear, cool freshness.
Above: different tones of the same grey have been washed
on the walls and the woodwork to increase
the sense of space.*

Deco

Two layers of ragged colour, silvery grey over charcoal, add up to a strongly textured background colour, a chic foil for the assorted Art Deco-style finishes in this fashionable living room. Flicking paint in a light on dark grey softens the severity of an Odeon-style fire place, metallic powders give a pewtery lustre to a mirror frame, and prosaic Hammerite gives a cheap clock a new lease of life. Too much grey could be melancholy- splashes of orange are the antidote, plus shiny chrome and gleaming black.

Bold swirls of ragged colour combine light and dark grey in tune with furnishing fashion. The colour and design are echoed by the abstract shape of the pottery vase. Flashes of burnt orange highlight the otherwise restrained scheme which is giiven necessary warmth by the wood floor.

Ragging-off

Ragging is one of the most popular and stylish of the currently fashionable paint finishes. Depending on the colours chosen and the type of glaze used, ragged walls can look softly blurry or crisply marked, like crushed velvet or even like marble, as in the thirties-style sitting room shown on the previous page. This was done in two stages with two coats of glaze, using alkyd semigloss paint thinned with paint thinner, with scumble glaze added to delay drying. This finish complements other typically thirties' textures in the room, like chrome, lacquer and metallic finishes, and helps soften a scheme which could otherwise look severe.

Soft and irregular ragging is achieved by frequently rearranging the rags during application.

Traditional ragging, also called ragging off, or scumbling, is an age-old artists' trick for breaking up a wet paint surface rapidly to give texture. Marblers and grainers also use rags, dabbed quickly over surfaces, to soften and disperse a glazed surface. Ragging off on walls is done more systematically, taking advantage of the attractive folded petal effects which, by pressing a bunched handful of rags into a wet glaze, are produced with wonderful ease. Another method of ragging is 'ragging on', where the rag is dipped in glaze and dabbed on to a dry base coat, giving the wall surface a variety of effects from swirls to softly printed patterns. Ragging off is easier if two people are doing it together: one applying the glaze and the other following with rags. For both methods, the rags must be lint-free – old, torn-up sheets are excellent. Some painters like to use different textures to alter the ragged surface subtly. Chamois leather makes strong, definite prints, interfacing makes crisp, fine ones, while coarse-textured fabric, such as burlap (washed well first) gives a woven texture.

Ragging techniques can also be used on furniture, either simply as an attractive finish, or – if walls are ragged as well – to blend an unsightly fitting or bulky object into the overall theme of the room. One of the reasons why special paint finishes have become so popular with do-it-yourselfers is that they provide such a useful means of incorporating furniture or built-in cabinets into a decorative scheme. Covering these items with plain paint tends to make them too obtrusive, and, though papering them can look pretty, the paper soon gets shabby and sometimes peels off. Given the same finish as walls, awkward furniture becomes almost invisible, which always helps to make a room look unified, and creates a more open, spacious feel.

Ragged walls and surfaces can look equally good in stylish modern interiors (left) as in cosier, more traditional rooms (below). The cupboard panels and drawer fronts of this dining room have been ragged, while the remaining wood has been either dragged, grained or marbled as required. The same colour paint, treated in different ways, has been used in this room as a means of unifying several large, disparate pieces of furniture, and by virtue of using a relatively pale shade, making them look less obtrusive.

Technique

There are two forms of ragging: 'ragging on', which is very similar to sponging (see page 116) and 'ragging off', an adaptation of rag rolling, where the rags are run over a wet glaze to create pattern by removing rather than applying colour. This room was decorated in the second way, using two shades of grey for a subtle, silvery finish to complement the furnishings. You need neither skill nor specialized equipment for this technique, but it is important to use a solvent-based paint for the base and a top coat made from 70 per cent scumble glaze, 20 per cent alkyd semigloss paint and 10 per cent paint thinner, mixed together in a paint bucket. You can buy scumble glaze, also called transparent oil glaze, from speciality paint companies or you can make your own, using equal parts of boiled linseed oil, turpentine and drying agent, plus a little whiting (about one tablespoon per quart). You can get by with alkyd semigloss paint in place of glaze for the simplest paint treatments like sponging and ragging on, but it's vital to use this mixture when rag rolling, ragging off and dragging. Why? Because these are techniques where you need to keep a 'wet edge' going and paint alone dries faster than you can work. Scumble or transparent oil glaze delays drying and gives you scope to achieve the effect you want. Remember that you'll need to allow more time for the walls to dry, especially if you use a home-made glaze made with linseed oil which may still be tacky after ten days.

1

Start by painting the walls with solvent-based paint and allow to dry.

Apply the first strip of glaze (70 per cent scumble glaze, 20 per cent solvent-based semigloss, 10 per cent paint thinner) using the 3 or 4 inch paintbrush so that the background is covered.

2

Work from the top of the wall down, painting strips from 18 to 36 inches wide. Start with a narrow width if this is your first attempt at the technique or if you are working alone.

3

Take the bunch of rags and dab or roll over the wet surface, starting from the top and working downwards. Changing the angle of your hand slightly will help to vary the pattern.

When you have reached the baseboard, start again from the top. Overlap the first strip slightly but take care to avoid a heavy build-up of paint. Continue applying glaze and ragging it off until the room is complete.

When the first coat is dry, apply the second layer of glaze in strips as before. Don't worry if you seem to be obliterating all your hard work; the original coat will be revealed when you rag over the glaze.

Take a clean bunch of rags rolled up into a loose sausage and work from the top to the bottom of the wall, overlapping the strips. You will remove enough glaze to reveal the first, darker coat, but the top coat will produce a toning sheen which lightens the effect.

Do's and Don'ts

DO ... use glaze, not paint alone, to keep a wet edge going.

... enlist some help if you are decorating a large room, so that as one of you applies the glaze, the other rags it off.

... experiment with different cloths to find the texture you want.

... throw the rags away when they become clogged with paint BUT take great care of how you dispose of them. Put them in an airtight container, *not* a plastic bag, as the rags are highly combustible and may ignite in three minutes on a hot day.

DON'T ... tackle too large an area at a time.

... work too slowly, or the effect may be patchy.

... forget to touch in or wipe off excess glaze at baseboard level, where a build-up may occur.

... worry about producing a perfect finish. It's the overall effect which counts, not the detail.

Equipment

You will need:
- solvent-based paint for the base coat.
- a roller or paintbrush for applying it.
- a bunch of rags – chamois leather, jersey or lint-free cotton – loosely wrapped into a sausage shape.
- glaze/paint/paint thinner mixture in two shades (we used charcoal topped by silver grey).
- a paint bucket.
- a 3 or 4 inch paintbrush.

Metallic Finishes

A glint of gold or silver introduced into a special paint finish not only makes it more dramatic, it also adds a really professional touch to the work. Metallic oxide powders come in a wide range of types — bronze, gold, silver and copper — and shades of colour as well. Surprisingly, perhaps, they're neither expensive nor particularly difficult to use. They lend themselves especially well to random effects, spattered or flicked on to a prepared adhesive surface. They can be used successfully in conjunction with stencils, as they were on Victorian papier-mâché ware, for borders, highlights and outlines. For stencilling, size is used to make the powder stick to the surface being treated. With this metallic mirror frame, however, tinted scumble glaze — painted in patterns over the frame — is used as the 'adhesive'. The powder, scattered over the frame, sticks to the tacky glaze and emphasizes the patterns. More texture is created with sprinkled drops of paint thinner, giving a pitted effect. When the glaze is dry, the frame is varnished over to protect this unusual iridescent finish.

1

All that glitters grew on trees! Metallic oxide mirror frame and fake fireplace are made from plywood, while the art deco-style clock's wooden case has been given a coat of hammered enamel in silver-grey to harmonize with its surroundings.

2

Prepare the mirror frame and prime if necessary, then paint with solvent-based paint and allow to dry.

Lay the frame flat. Take the larger paintbrush and daub on splodges of the darker glaze in bold, irregular strokes. Don't cover the base paint completely; the glazed patches should link but they should not obliterate the background.

3

Take the smaller paintbrush and apply the lighter glaze in the same way while the dark glaze is still tacky. Allow it to overlap the dark patches but leave some areas where the dark glaze shows through.

Fold the cloth into a compact bundle and roll it over the wet surface, blending the two colours to create a mottled background.

Dip the finer of the two artists' brushes into the metallic powder. Hold it about an inch away from the frame and tap it gently with your forefinger so that the powder falls in small, irregular heaps. Treat a small area and then follow step 5.

Dip the larger artists' brush in paint thinner. Hold it slightly higher than last time and, supporting it on a piece of wood, tap it so that drops scatter over the powdered area, creating a pitted effect.

Repeat steps 4 and 5 until you have finished the frame, allow to dry and coat with clear varnish.

4

5

6

Technique

The glitter of metallic powder makes this the perfect paint treatment to accompany chrome and steel. It can turn an old or undistinguished frame, shelf or table-top into a piece that's decorative as well as functional, but there are limits to its use. Because the technique involves scattering metallic powder on to wet glaze, it should be applied to horizontal rather than vertical surfaces. This rules out doors, unless you can be bothered to take them off their hinges and rehang them, and chairs and tables too, unless you reserve the treatment for the seat or top. You'll need to turn cupboards from side to side to treat each plane separately so it's best to reserve this treatment for small pieces of furniture or accessories, like the mirror frame shown here.

Equipment

You will need:
- solvent-based semigloss paint for the base coat.
- two batches of glaze mix made from 50 per cent scumble (transparent oil) glaze and 50 per cent solvent-based semigloss paint. (We used black and grey).
- superfine metallic powder, available from art shops.
- two standard paintbrushes (we used 1 and 2 inch).
- two artists' paintbrushes (we used sable nos. 6 and 8).
- a clean cotton cloth.
- paint thinner.
- clear varnish.
- a varnish brush or a clean paintbrush.

Flicking & Spattering

Vividly reminiscent of the action paintings of the fifties, flicking and spattering gives furniture a stunning look that's right for today's styles. Any surrounding areas you want to keep plain must be masked off carefully, because flicked paint can go astray. Apart from this preliminary precaution, flicking and spattering provide a fast method of jazzing up plain surfaces, and if the colours are well chosen the final effect can be highly sophisticated. Flicking produces wilder markings, zig-zags and squiggles, while spattering builds up a 'pointilliste' texture of dots and spots of colour which can be sparsely scattered or as close-textured as granite.

The spattering technique can be applied equally well with fabric paints to produce a co-ordinated look.

Flicking is a form of spattering that's especially suited to a thirties, fifties – or eighties – style setting. The appeal of these finishes lies partly in their random quality, an air of not having been laboriously worked over. The two techniques are similar but applied in slightly different ways to vary the effect. Flicking is wilder than spattering, which is done in a rather more controlled fashion.

Spattering creates a shower of fine dots which looks equally attractive on large areas, like walls, or small pieces, like china. The best results are achieved with several colours (two tones of one colour plus a darker one for emphasis) on a white or pale ground. Use latex paint on walls, enamel for china or glass, thinned with the appropriate agent if necessary to obtain spots rather than splodges. Use a wide (3 or 4 inch) wall brush for large areas or an artists' brush for tiny items, tapped sharply against a piece of wood so that paint sprays out on to the surface. It will spray on to other surfaces too, of course, so mask off any areas you want to keep clear and treat portable pieces in the garage or outside on a still day.

Flicking is less subtle. Here you positively want the runs you need to avoid when spattering. Resist the temptation to thin the paint too much and concentrate on technique instead, jerking your wrist to produce squiggles of paint. You can only successfully flick horizontal surfaces, as excessively long runs will form on vertical ones, and it's better tried on substantial areas rather than small. We used a fake fireplace cut from plywood to give interest to this featureless room, but you could flick or spatter an existing fireplace, using a heat-resistant paint (see page 72).

Equipment

To paint our plywood fake you will need:

- primer.
- solvent-based semigloss paint for the base coat.
- latex paint or alkyd-based paint thinned with paint thinner for flicking.
- 3 and ¾ inch paintbrushes.

1

Apply primer, followed by at least two coats of solvent-based semigloss paint, using the larger paintbrush.

When the final base coat is dry, dip the ¾ inch brush into the latex paint, thinned with water if necessary. (If it's too thick it will splat rather than flick. Experiment on a piece of newspaper until you find the right consistency.) With a deft movement of your wrist, flick the paint at random over the background.

2

When you have flicked the entire surface, step back to examine the effect. Fill in any obvious gaps by flicking in the same way.

Hammered enamel clock

The deco-style clock is coated with a metallic treatment that needs no mixing or preparation. Hammered enamel finish is sprayed on straight from the can and needs no primer or under-coat. Originally developed for use on metal, it's suitable for decorative woodwork, lightly sanded so it will adhere, though it's not recommended for exterior use. It is available in a range of metallic colours and has the con-sistency of conventional paint un-til it is painted on to the surface when it pickles to give the charac-teristic hammered finish.

3

The finished flicked 'fireplace' shows how effective this freehand technique can be. Colours are restricted to black and white for emphasis and the shape was deliberately chosen to echo the effect of the clock, a period (time) piece.

Country Style

Gentle, cheering apricot, the colour of afternoon sunshine, dapples the sponged walls of this pretty, countrified bedroom and offsets the rustic simplicity of bare colourwashed boards, frosty white quilt and muslin drapes. The vigorously folksy painted chest has curlicues of colour created by a blob of modelling clay pressed into a home-made vinegar glaze. Sponging is a finish to have fun with, and its artless texture suits small rooms with low ceilings and deep-set cottage windows. Wooden doors are colour rubbed to blend in, and a tiny cast iron grate has been 'antiqued' to bring out the elaborate design.

Apricot and honey sponged over ivory give the walls a warm wash of colour. The simplicity of the decoration is emphasized by the furnishings.

Sponging

Sponging colour on to walls or furniture
is one of the quickest and easiest ways of creating a
soft, dappled effect. The only equipment you need
is a sea-sponge, preferably one with a good holey
texture. You can create a wide variety of effects —
sponging light colours over a darker base, or dark
over light; you can go for strong contrasts or close
harmonies; and you can achieve very dense
surfaces or light, airy ones. It's equally suited to
country cottages or to urban surroundings,
especially if a tough solvent-based paint is used.
Varnished over to seal the finish, sponging looks,
and stays looking good in bathrooms,
kitchens and hallways.

*Baseboard and walls are both sponged to produce an effect
that is sophisticated and yet artless.*

The origins of sponged effects are lost in the anonymous byways of folk art, where many such methods were used both for speed and simplicity, and because they created effects comparable to sophisticated techniques like marbling and graining.

Today sponging is probably one of the most popular special paint finishes — its informality suits contemporary furnishing styles, and it is disarmingly simple to achieve.

Technique

First, choose your sponge. You need for this technique a crisp, medium-size sea sponge — too small and it will make the wall look spotty, though tiny sponges are useful for treating picture frames and the like.

Before you begin, soak the sponge in water and wring out well to avoid thinning the paint or you'll get drips and runs. This keeps the sponge pliable and fluffy. Sponging is one technique where you can use semigloss finish latex both as a base coat and for the treatment itself, but remember that it will dry quickly and give a more defined effect than solvent-based paint or a tinted glaze.

Try the technique on a piece of paper first until you are satisfied with the effect. Don't overload the sponge, or you will produce patchy areas and possibly runs. Keep the rhythm of prints flowing fairly evenly across the wall surface. Random heavy build-ups of prints in one spot tend to look blotchy. It's important to change the way you hold your hand and to turn the sponge as you go to avoid too directional a pattern; if you find the effect is too regular, tear the sponge open and continue, using the cut edge.

Sponging should look cloudy and delicate. Using two colours

gives more subtle results than one, which may produce too marked a contrast with the base coat. Let plenty of background show through when you apply the first coat, for an open effect, but make sure you overlap the second coat so that all three colours merge. It's safest to choose colours which blend for your early attempts and to leave contrasts until you have mastered the technique. Either apply two darker colours over a pale base, as here, or start with a deep base coat and lighten the effect with progressively paler colours sponged over the top.

Do's and Don'ts

DO ... use a natural sea sponge.

... choose pastels, unless you are very confident about your choice of colour.

... keep a sheet of paper by you to experiment on and to check the effect every time you reload the sponge.

... remember to vary the way you hold the sponge.

DON'T ... use a wet sponge, or the paint will run.

... overload the sponge.

... blot out too much of the background.

... omit features like radiators and cupboards, which can be camouflaged if sponged to match the walls.

Equipment

You will need:

● latex, or solvent-based paint, for the base coat.

● a roller or paintbrush for applying the base coat.

● a medium-size sea sponge.

● latex, solvent-based semigloss paint or glaze in two colours for sponging.

● a paint tray.

● a rag for wiping away splashes, soaked in paint thinner (for solvent-based paint) or detergent solution (for latex).

1

2

3

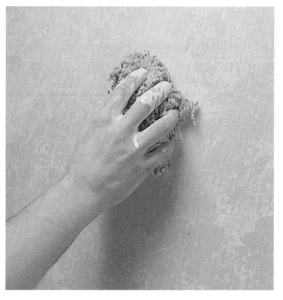

Paint the walls with the base colour of your choice (we used ivory for a delicate effect) and allow to dry. Pour a little paint or glaze (see recipe on page 108) for sponging into the tray, dip the sponge into it and remove the excess on the ribbed slope.

Starting at the top of the wall, dab quickly in a random direction, reloading the sponge and changing its direction until the wall is covered. Allow to dry.

Apply the second colour in the same way, overlapping with the first.

Continue until the wall is complete, merging the two colours but allowing the background to show through.

*Sponging is one of the most versatile
paint treatments. Use it to blend
woodwork with walls and drapes
(right) or in contrasting panels to
help break up and give interest to
large areas (below). Two shades of
grey on cream are used here to
co-ordinate with the glossy black
furniture and the panels are edged
with wooden moulding, painted to
match the baseboard. In contrast the
grey panel on the wall (far right)
seems to merge with its surround.
Marked by two black slats, it has a
crisp even texture which adds
interest without seeming to
encroach on space.*

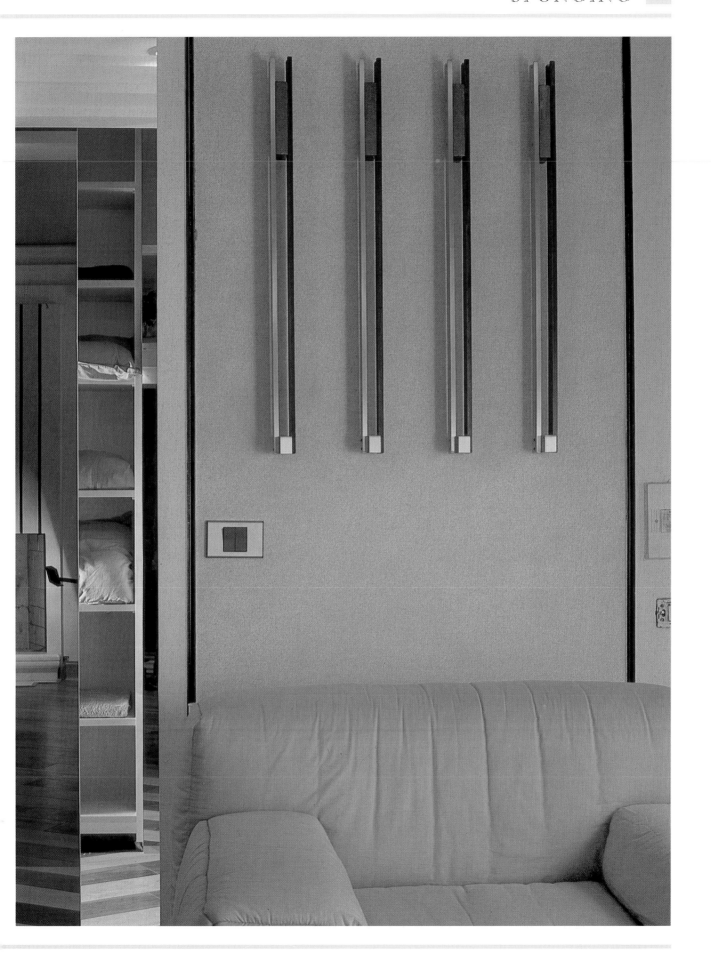

Colour Rubbing

A traditional method of emphasizing
the contours of any relief moulding in a room, or
on furniture, is to brush a dark-toned glaze over it
and then, after leaving this to set for a short time,
rub it away on the prominent parts. This mimics
the effect of use and time and deepens the contrast
of highlights and shadows. It can also add interest
to a highly decorative cast-iron Victorian
fireplace, like the one shown here, to bring out the
intricacy of its design.
Colour washing, used below on the floorboards
also has the effect of conferring something akin to
the patina of age on newly stripped soft wood as
well as softening its colour.

*Fireplace and doors are colour rubbed and floorboards
colourwashed in apricot to blend with the bedroom walls.*

Colour washing bare, wood plank floors has become quite popular as a way of softening the yellowy tinge of stripped soft wood. The technique involves brushing a milky-coloured glaze or thin wash of water-based paint (either method can be used successfully, though both need varnishing over for protection) over the surface needing improvement. Most standard floorboards are made from soft wood planking, and have been for over a century. Unsealed, they rapidly becomes grubby and discoloured; sealed, their basically gingery tone is unpleasantly emphasized. So a greyish-white glaze brushed over the bare wood, and then sealed in, is a simple corrective. Curiously enough, the effect of colour-washed floors is very similar to the look of boards well sanded and scoured – which was actually the standard eighteenth-century finish for most wood floors. Though it's common to imagine old oak floors as darkly gleaming with years of polishing, around two hundred years ago the practice was to scour them frequently with wet sand and herbs, which not only left them smelling sweet but also smoothed the grain and softened it to a gentle, silvery grey. This remedy was practised in large country homes, as well as in rural cottages.

Greyed boards make a very attractive background for floor stencils, since they are sufficiently uniform in tone to make the pattern stand out, but varied enough – due to the changing wood grain – to be lively. A charming example to be seen in an Irish country house bedroom uses a simple repeating motif in dull blue over the greyed floor, with a border all round the edge in the same blue. Even without a rug, the patterned floor looks both elegant and welcoming.

In the cottage bedroom shown here, the 'time-worn' effect of the colour-washed floorboards is suitably enhanced by the 'antiqued' pine doors.

Technique

The aim of colour rubbing is to produce a faded, weathered look which emphasizes mouldings and areas of high relief and deepens shadows. To do this you literally rub colour away, so it's important to start with a deep shade or the effect may disappear completely. You'll need a thicker glaze than for most paint treatments (75 per cent scumble glaze, 20 per cent paint and a very small amount of thinner – 5 per cent is quite enough), brushed into the surface so that all the crevices are filled. Wait until the glaze begins to dry but is tacky to the touch before you begin to rub it; too soon and you will remove most of the glaze, too late and it will come away in patches. It's worth experimenting on a scrap of wood before you start so that you have some idea of the colour you'll achieve, but remember that different surfaces will give different effects. In most cases it's best to apply a base coat of alkyd semigloss before you start so that the glaze is not absorbed. As this is not a fine finish, it can be applied to bare wood, provided this has been made slippery with paint thinner, and you are prepared to ignore minor irregularities, but porous areas of filled plaster will soak up colour and will look all too noticeable unless sealed.

Equipment

You will need:
- alkyd semigloss for the base coat.
- a brush or roller.
- thick glaze, as above.
- a paintbrush and paint bucket.
- plenty of lint-free rags.

1

Start by preparing the surface. The cast-iron fireplace was scoured thoroughly with a wire brush, wiped clean, and painted with metal primer. It was then given two coats of undercoat and a base coat of alkyd semigloss. The doors were stripped and sanded and wiped with paint thinner.

Mix up the glaze in a paint bucket and apply with a brush, working well into the mouldings.

2

When the glaze begins to harden, take a soft cloth and rub over the surface with a circular movement. Don't try to clean out the crevices; these should remain as areas of shadow.

3

The same treatment may be used on doors or walls. On wood, apply the glaze and rub off along the grain, treating panels before mouldings. On plaster, use a circular movement but don't attempt to achieve an even finish – the idea is to create a modern fresco effect.

Vinegar Graining

Vinegar graining, or putty graining, as it is sometimes called, is said to have been invented by an American firm of furniture makers in the mid-nineteenth century. By stamping and rolling pieces of linseed oil putty over a simple glaze made from powdered colour and ordinary household vinegar with a little sugar added for 'stick', they found they could produce boldly grained and tigerishly-striped effects on furniture with a minimum of effort. It was also discovered that because of the way oil and vinegar naturally repel each other, attractive secondary patterns emerged of their own accord, making 'designs' like ferns or seaweed fronds.

A cheap occasional table, rescued from a junkshop, has been colour co-ordinated to match the chest at the foot of the bed.

The early American furniture makers impressed all sorts of found objects on their vinegar glazes, creating interesting patterns quickly. Fans of paper for example, pressed down for a moment, leave a distinct fan-shaped mark – useful for filling corners on a chest or highboy. Dried corn cobs, corks and leaves can also be used to make patterns, as well as the more traditional putty, squeezed into blobs or sausages. A lump of putty – or modelling clay – dragged along in a spiral shape leaves a fascinating, bold pattern like thick rope. The only problem with this appealingly easy technique is knowing when to stop! Care must be taken to let the finished piece dry thoroughly and not worry when – like a wet pebble – the wonderful shapes and markings tend to fade as the glaze dries. Once dry, however, a quick coat of gloss varnish brings them vividly to life again. Varnishing is essential to fix and protect a glaze like this, which otherwise would simply wash off again. Two to three coats of varnish, applied in dust-free conditions and rubbed down gently in between, will give a tough washable finish, besides adding a patina which gives any vinegar-glazed piece the look of an early American antique.

Technique

This is a brash, primitive finish to have fun with, using combs, modelling clay, paper or thumb prints to create pattern on a beer or vinegar-and-water glaze. Although you have time to experiment with materials and design and you can cover quite a large area before the glaze sets, it looks best restricted to small areas of half a square yard or so. It's important to have some idea of the pattern you want and how you intend to go about it before you start, so set aside some time for a few practice runs on paper. Before you begin you'll need to paint the surface with a solvent-based semigloss paint pale enough to show up the vinegar-glaze markings. Rub down when dry with silicon carbide (wet and dry) abrasive paper to remove the shine. Then wipe the surface clean with a cloth wrung out in plain vinegar or beer before applying the glaze. The glaze itself is made from half a cup of malt vinegar mixed with a teaspoon of sugar (helps this medicine stay down) and a squeeze of dishwashing detergent. Place some powder paint, either artists' pigment or children's poster paint, in a second bowl or jar and add enough vinegar solution to form a paste. Now add the rest of the vinegar and mix together thoroughly. Test the glaze on a piece of paper before you start and hold it upright to see if the colour runs. If it does it is too thick. Add more vinegar until the right consistency is obtained. This treatment won't withstand hard wear, so when you have applied and decorated the glaze you'll need to finish it with a coat of polyurethane varnish or wax polish.

Equipment

You will need:
- solvent-based semigloss paint for the base coat.
- a 2 inch paintbrush for applying it.
- silicon carbide (wet and dry) abrasive paper.
- plain malt vinegar (available in most supermarkets).
- lint-free cloth.
- vinegar glaze (see recipe above).
- a 2 inch brush for applying it.
- modelling clay.
- varnish or wax polish.

1

2

3

The vigorous pattern on this chest was made by whorls of modelling clay rolled around on the vinegar glaze. The bedside table was treated in the same way for instant co-ordination.

First paint the surface with solvent-based semigloss paint. Rub down when dry to remove the sheen. Wipe with plain vinegar or beer and apply the vinegar glaze. Leave until it is tacky, and while it is drying form the modelling clay into different shapes and experiment with the patterns on a piece of paper.

Roll the modelling clay over the vinegar glaze to give the spiral motif shown here. Dabbing or pressing it into the glaze gives a different effect and crumpled paper and thumb prints also work well.

Rural Retreat

Red is a make-or-break colour in decorating unless, as in this cockle-warming country kitchen, its inherent fieriness is tempered by layering glaze in different tones of transparent red, a clever treatment that makes for depth and richness without glare. Stippling each coat of glaze softens the colour to a suede-like bloom. Dark oak and a collection of blue and white pottery, old and new, stand out vividly against warm red walls, and a rustic floor of combed blue-on-blue squares repeats the colour contrast in a quieter key.

Fine stippling over large areas like walls may be time-consuming but well worth the effort — witness the welcoming glow produced here. While plain furniture highlights the decorative finish, kitchen cabinets have been dragged in the same colour glaze to give a sense of unity.

Stippling

Stippling a wet glaze breaks up the colour into myriads of tiny dots, and when dry this presents a softened, smooth-looking flow of colour, with a texture reminiscent of airbrushing. It is a technique known to artists from centuries back, and used wherever the need arose for a fine surface bloom of colour which allowed the base tint beneath to 'breathe' through, as it were. Stippling is also particularly useful for blurring the demarcation line between two separate fields of colour so that they merge imperceptibly into each other. This quality was often used in thirties' decorating schemes based on graduated bands of stippled colours across walls and ceilings.

Like sponging and ragging, stippling produces the broken colour particularly attractive when used as a background.

In appearance, stippling is first cousin to sponging: it can even be done with a sponge. The important difference is that it is carried out on wet glaze, so that colour is removed rather than added. It's easier if there are two of you, one to apply the glaze and the other to stipple, especially if you are using a stippling brush which is relatively small scale.

Proper stippling brushes are square-shaped, with pads of soft thick bristles – usually badger hair because its split ends hold more colour. They are also rather expensive. For large areas, a proper stippling brush, with its larger pad of bristles and solid handle, is probably a sensible investment because it undoubtedly is the right tool for the job. But for smaller surfaces such as furniture, or for one small room, it's not essential to use a purpose-made stippling brush. You can compromise with a dusting brush, a shoe brush, a hair brush or even a broom, as long as you are prepared to cut the bristles to an even length – a tapered brush won't do. For speed, especially when working alone, consider using a mohair or lambswool roller which will leave a softer, less defined pattern, a sponge (sea or cellulose) or rags, but don't expect the same precision that a stippling brush gives.

Traditionally stippling is carried out on a coloured glaze applied over a white ground but it's just as attractive using deeper, related colours. Decorators often stipple strong colours – like the warm red on our country kitchen walls – to soften their impact, especially when they have been applied as here over a paler base colour.

In rooms where the walls need occasional washing down, a stippled finish should be sealed with at least one coat of varnish.

Technique

The base coat should be solvent-based semigloss paint, and the glaze is the usual 70 percent scumble, 20 percent alkyd semigloss, 10 percent paint thinner mix. Try it out on small areas, and start in one corner of the window wall (where there is less direct light to show up flaws) and from there keep on until you reach another corner. Whether you're tackling walls or woodwork, remember to treat the side opposite, not next to, the one you stippled first or you may smear the work you thought was complete.

Do's and Don'ts

DO ... work in strips, no more than a yard wide.
... stipple in a vertical direction.
... use a firm, even touch when applying the stippling brush.
... clean the brush, sponge or roller and change the rags frequently to avoid a build-up of paint.
DON'T ... stop in the middle of a wall and allow the glaze to dry, or the seam will show.
... try to stipple latex paint with a brush – it dries too quickly. (But you can use a roller or a sponge.)
... use a foam roller – it will spread, rather than dapple, the glaze.

Equipment

For classical stippling you will need:
● alkyd semigloss for the base coat.
● a roller and paint tray for applying it.
● glaze, as above.
● a paint bucket.
● a 3 or 4 inch wall brush for applying the glaze.
● a stippling brush.
● paint thinner and rags for cleaning the brush.

1

The base coat should be an opaque, even colour or the delicate stippling will not show. Paint the surface with one or two coats of alkyd semigloss, and allow to dry.

Apply the glaze in strips as shown, working from the top of the wall down. Narrow strips, about 18 inches wide, are best if you are stippling with a brush, but you can increase this to an arm's width across if you are using a roller.

2

Take the stippling brush and apply it to the glaze with a deft, positive movement, taking care not to cause streaks or runs. Repeat until the entire strip is stippled. In a room like this kitchen, it's a good idea to finish with a protective coat of polyurethane varnish when the stippling is dry.

3

Stippling gives a glow which softens the depth of the brick red paint, chosen to contrast with the blue and white china and floor tiles and to add warmth to this cottage kitchen.

Combing

Combing, as the name suggests, is a decorative technique which consists of raking a comb with widely-spaced teeth through wet paint to make regularly spaced stripes, or patterns. Grainers often use special steel graining combs, in various sizes and spacings, to imitate the grain in coarse-textured woods like oak. Combing is an effective and quick way to add surface interest to large painted areas such as floors, but for the combing to register from eye-level, the comb teeth need to be extra widely-spaced. Some wooden Afro combs do the trick quite well; alternatively you could make an improvised 'comb' by cutting regular V-shaped nicks into a rubber window-cleaning squeegee — this is easier to use because of its solid handle. To show up clearly, the combed colour needs to be contrasted with the base colour: either tone on tone, as with the blue on blue floor in this country kitchen (inspired by the blue china and pottery), or in a colour over white. For a really jazzy version go for a Deco-style colour contrast — shocking pink or silver over black, perhaps.

1

Remember that bare wood must be thoroughly sanded, cleaned and primed. Then apply undercoat and several coats of alkyd semigloss paint for a uniform colour and allow to dry. Now brush the paint for combing over the first tile.

Start at the edge of the tile and pull the comb of your choice across the paint. It's easier to start with relatively straight lines at first until you gauge the effect, but don't worry if they are not absolutely even.

2

Now be creative! You can comb straight lines in the opposite direction, change combs to vary the effect, or use sweeping strokes to form curves. Though the tiles need not be identical, the floor should, however, have some coherence when complete. When the paint is dry, install the floor tiles and coat with at least three layers of varnish, adding a little white gloss or alkyd semigloss if you want to prevent yellowing.

3

Adapt the pattern to suit the area to be covered. Stiff steel combs create regular waves; on this tile the impression is similar to watered silk.

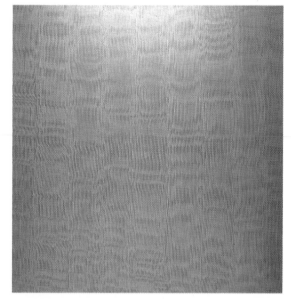

Pliable rubber combs can be used to form the fish-scale curves shown here.

Diagonal lines suit a formal or modern setting and can give a mock wood-grained effect.

4

5

6

A combed floor, in fresh attractive colours, makes a cheap and cheerful alternative to the more usual vinyl.

Technique

This is one treatment where you can use paint straight from the can, latex or alkyd semigloss or gloss, though it's still important to use a non-absorbent solvent-based paint for the base coat so that the comb slithers about satisfactorily. If you want to thin the top coat, use about 25 per cent paint thinner (or water if using latex) to 75 per cent paint, but make sure that it is thick enough to give adequate coverage.

It's easier to treat plywood tiles before they are laid (for instructions on levelling the floor surface and cutting see pages 78-9 and 96. The tiles should be glued as well as tacked at the corners. If you are treating floorboards, divide the floor into areas approximately 2 feet square to give a mock tiled effect, and if it's a room you can't shut the door on until the floor is dry – a hall, for instance – comb every other square so that you leave a series of stepping stones for access. Remember to finish the floor with as many coats of heavy-duty polyurethane varnish as you can apply; a minimum of three is required to protect the finish.

Equipment

You will need:
● sufficient solvent-based paint to give an opaque, even base coat.
● a wall brush or roller for applying it.
● alkyd or latex semigloss paint for combing.
● a paintbrush for applying the top coat.
● graining combs or substitutes.
● heavy-duty polyurethane varnish for at least three coats.

Border Country

The simplest decorating ideas can be the most effective. An update of that favourite trick of thirties decor, walls enlivened by 'panels' cut from contrasting wallpapers, adds colour and interest to this friendly, flowery living room while unobtrusively emphasizing its period detail and proportions. Shelves and cupboard doors are two-tone painted to match the predominant colours of pale lilac and primrose. A small bamboo table, painted white and bamboo 'striped' in coloured glaze, is promoted from junk to pretty pedestal for a great bowl of flowering plants.

Precisely placed panels can balance the proportions of any room. Here an open leafy design is used as a background with a darker companion print in the centre of the panels, edged with the same pattern in yellow.

Paper Panelling

Cutting wallpaper into 'panels' scaled to a room's proportions, and pasting them down with a decorative paper border, is such a simple idea that you'll be surprised to find how effective it looks. For some reason, subdividing blank walls into panels makes a room look satisfyingly composed, especially if it is featureless to start with. Also, of course, it can add colour and pattern in manageable doses — useful at the early stage of homemaking when most people are short of pictures and decorative bits and pieces to fill up bare spaces. Once the 'panel' system has been worked out, cutting and pasting is easy.

Borders and friezes are chosen carefully to suit the style of a room, perhaps emphasizing a pattern (below), motif (top right) or colour scheme (bottom right).

There are so many borders and friezes available now that you're spoilt for choice if you want to recreate this paper panelled room. Widths range from about ¾ to 18 inches, and though most require pasting in the same way as wallpaper, you'll also find ready-pasted wallpaper or vinyl and polyethylene borders, where you paste the wall.

Technique

Whether you are attaching a border or making a panel, you must mark the horizontal and check it with a spirit level. Measure and mark the wall in several places and join the marks with a chalk line. Step back to assess the effect. If it looks crooked even though you're sure it's straight, the chances are that the baseboard or moulding is out of true. In this case, adjust the level until the line appears straight, whether it is or not. Now apply adhesive to the border (ordinary wallpaper paste for wallpaper, heavy-duty for vinyl), moisten the back of a ready-pasted frieze to activate the paste or paste a band of adhesive on the wall for polyethylene. Concertina long lengths of frieze and paste on to the wall, following your guideline, pressing into place with a smoothing brush. Butt join the ends where necessary, ensuring that the pattern matches. Remove any adhesive on the face of the border and run a seam roller over it, paying particular attention to the edges.

To make a paper panel you will need to draw a box, using a spirit level and plumb line to establish the horizontal and vertical. Cut and paste a similar-sized section of wallpaper to form the centre of the panel, smooth into place and trim if necessary. Paste a length of border along the first vertical, allowing 1 inch more than you require at each end, then smooth

the first horizontal piece of border into place, allowing a similar margin. Now mitre the corner: place a steel rule or straight edge across the diagonal from the outer to the inner edge and cut along this line with a trimming knife. Remove the excess triangle on top, then peel back the horizontal border and take away the second piece of surplus underneath. Smooth the edges down and repeat until all four corners are mitred.

·Do's and Don'ts

DO ... spend time marking out where all the panels will be before you start. Make mock panels to judge the effect if necessary.
... check the horizontal and vertical and adjust to suit.
... use the appropriate paste.
... mitre the corners.
DON'T ... paste borders on to relief (such as embossed) wallpaper unless you are sure they will stick.
... butt join corners.
... forget about pattern matching when you join lengths.
... use a seam roller over an embossed frieze; it will crush the pattern.

Equipment

For making paper panels you will need:
- a spirit level and plumb line.
- wallpaper and co-ordinating border.
- scissors.
- the appropriate paste (or water for ready-pasted varieties).
- a paintbrush or sponge for applying paste (most pasting brushes are too wide).
- a smoothing brush.
- a straight edge.
- a trimming knife.
- a damp sponge for removing excess paste.
- a seam roller.

Bambooing

Bambooing, as a lighthearted method of simulating the rings and markings of bamboo in paint, seems to have been developed during the late eighteenth-century craze for exotic effects in decoration and furnishings. Elegant examples of painted bambooing can be seen in the Brighton Pavilion, where it was devised to suit rooms decorated in the Regency version of chinoiserie. The furniture was not made from real bamboo but of wood turned, carved and painted to imitate bamboo. The effect was so attractive it began to be copied and became a technique that has continued to this day among decorators and furniture restorers.

This 'bamboo' towel rail is actually made from turned wood, stained and painted to look like the real article.

You don't need bamboo to bamboo! It's a 'bamboozling' technique that's suitable for any turned or half-round (semi-circular) wood, and it looks just as effective in frankly fake colours like pink and cream as in a naturalistic yellowy-beige. What's important is to imitate the shading, spines and freckles associated with bamboo, especially the female bamboo, which is the type most often used as a model.

Technique

Furniture should be carefully prepared before you begin (see Basic Decorating Techniques pp. 58 to 61). Rub down real bamboo with denatured alcohol and steel wool, and if you want to preserve the natural colour, seal when dry with polyurethane varnish. Otherwise paint wood or bamboo with at least three coats of alkyd semigloss in the colour of your choice (this shade should be the lightest of those you use), sanding down with silicon carbide (wet and dry) abrasive paper and soapy water between each. Mottle the top coat with a rag while it is still damp for an attractive dappled effect. You will also need to think about colour for the details. It's usual to paint each stage slightly darker than the one before, so you will need three batches of glaze, though only a saucerful of each, and you can deepen the colour by adding more paint at each stage. When painting bamboo, be guided by its natural joints. You will have to decide where these are to go when painting turned wood, but it's a good idea to use any seams as a guide and to vary the placing for a more natural effect.

Do's and Don'ts

DO ... choose toning colours for the best effect.

... mottle the top coat to soften it slightly.

... decide where you want the 'joints' to go before you decorate wood.

... paint all the wide rings together, followed by the medium and narrow bands.

DON'T ... forget to obliterate the background with several coats of paint, unless you prefer to varnish natural bamboo.

... try to paint details with too large a brush.

... omit the final coat of varnish which protects the design.

... rush. This is a technique which demands care and time to look successful.

Equipment

You will need:

● sufficient alkyd semigloss for at least three base coats.

● a 1 inch paintbrush for applying it.

● silicon carbide paper and soapy water for rubbing down between base coats.

● a rag for mottling the finish.

● three batches of glaze in toning colours made from 70 percent scumble, 20 percent alkyd semigloss, 10 percent paint thinner.

● ¾-inch paintbrush for drawing the stripes.

● artists' brushes numbers 3 and 6 for painting details.

● polyurethane varnish.

1

Prepare and paint the piece as explained left and allow to dry.

Dip the ¾-inch paintbrush in the lightest batch of glaze and draw a wide (1¼-inch) band of watery colour round the bamboo or wood, centring it on the joint or where it might be. Repeat until all these rings are complete.

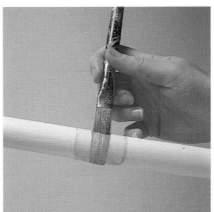

2

Tint the glaze with more paint so that it becomes a shade darker and draw a second band inside the first about ½ inch wide. Repeat until stage 2 is complete.

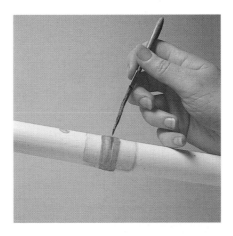

3

Add more paint to darken the glaze. Using the no. 3 artists' brush, draw a fine ring in the centre of the second band.

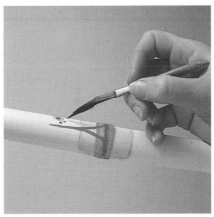

4

Take the no. 6 brush and mark in the spine and 'eyes'. Draw a V-shape about a third the diameter of the band in size and tail it off to form a point. Clean the brush and, with the first batch of colour, draw little ovals each side of the spine. Finish by adding tiny freckles in the darkest colour.

Water Colours

Stencilled decoration looks livelier against a background of subtly broken colour, and the shell designs used to pretty up the floor and old-fashioned tub here seem to have a natural affinity with the cloudy swirls of watery aquamarine colour washed over the walls of a fresh and pretty bathroom. More watery colour, in silvery grey, cools the gingery tone of soft wood planks to a subtle smoky shade. Waviness of a different, more formal kind, is introduced by the faux malachite finish on a plain mirror frame — elegant but remarkably easy to do.

Colour washing gives a broken colour, softer in effect than plain alkyd or latex paint. It forms a perfect background for more decorative finishes and is a practical choice for areas affected by condensation.

Stencilling

Stencils look especially effective against a softly distressed background, and colour washing makes the ideal foil. Against this watery seaside colour washing in aqua, stencilled sea shells look suitably marine, and pretty as well with their lacy shapes. The charm of stencils is that they are so versatile. This example shows them used as a border round pale-washed floorboards, delineating the washbasin, and as a decorative flourish on the underside of a traditional bath tub with claw feet. More sea shells are stencilled on the pale green cotton blind. Details like this cost next to nothing but add delightful character and professional polish to the simplest room.

Stencils provide an adaptable pattern which can mirror the contours of a room, as this sea shell design shows.

Stencils range from simple motifs in one colour to elaborate designs which require a separate stencil for every colour. They are cut from oiled cardboard or acetate, ready-made or adapted from an existing pattern. To cut your own stencils, it's often easier to trace a small-scale design and to have it enlarged on a photocopier. It's essential to provide sufficient 'bridges' to separate the painted areas, otherwise you will be left with a blob in place of the shape you had in mind! Make sure that the ties are not too thin or the stencil will be fragile and may break. Provided you've retained the original design you can always cut another stencil – but it is a nuisance.

Technique

When you are satisfied with the design, slip a sheet of carbon paper under the tracing and transfer it on to stencil card, or put acetate over the top and trace over the outline with a china-graph pencil. To cut round the outline you'll need a craft knife, and a board beneath. Leave a 2 inch border above and below the pattern to increase its strength. For painting you can use standard alkyd or latex paint, signwriters' paint which is thick and easy to manipulate, acrylic artists' paint or the spray paint designed for cars. The paint should be applied with a stubby stencil brush; don't overload it or the paint may run behind the stencil. Attach a stencil to the wall with masking tape or spray photo-mount, (don't press the stencil down hard or it will adhere completely), not adhesive gum which will make it stick out. If you are using the stencil for a frieze, mark the level before you begin, as it's only too easy to waver! You can create an interesting pattern by regularly reversing the stencil – as long as you clean the stencil first.

You can stencil on virtually any surface from plaster to wood or melamine (sanded so paint will adhere). This finish was tar-based, sealed with diluted pva adhesive and topped with two coats of alkyd semigloss to prevent the tar from bleeding through. Stencilling on fabric is no more difficult than stencilling on walls if you keep the fabric taut. Use special fabric paints which are heat-set by ironing when the pattern is complete so that they do not run when washed.

Do's and Don'ts

DO ... use oiled stencil cardboard or acetate which can be wiped clean.

... leave sufficient 'bridges' when adapting a design.

... use a stencil brush, not an ordinary paint or artists' brush.

... make sure the stencil is straight before you start to paint.

DON'T ... start with too ambitious a design (geometric or stylized designs are best).

... use paint that's too liquid in consistency.

... use adhesive gum to attach the stencil, or paint will bleed beneath.

... forget to clean the stencil before you reverse it.

Equipment

To cut a stencil from cardboard you will need:
- a stencil design on tracing paper, enlarged to the appropriate size.
- carbon paper and pencil.
- board or plywood to rest on.
- a craft knife and blades.
- stencil card.
- masking tape or spray photo-mount.
- paint (latex, alkyd, signwriters', acrylic or spray).
- a saucer for the paint.
- paint thinner (for cleaning).
- polyurethane varnish.

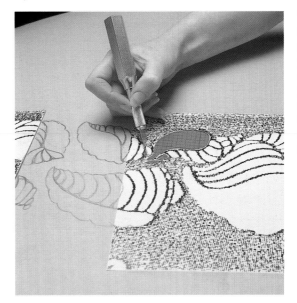

1

Transfer the design on to stencil card using the carbon paper and pencil. Place the stencil card over the board or plywood and carefully cut out the areas between ties with a craft knife, taking care not to break the 'bridges'.

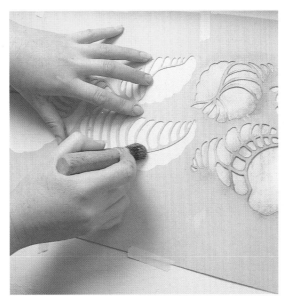

2

Attach the stencil on to the area to be painted with masking tape or spray photo-mount applied lightly. Pour a little paint into the saucer (we used signwriters' paint) and dab the stencil brush into it, working it into the bristles. Remove excess paint on a piece of paper, and holding the stencil in place with one hand, fill in the cut-outs with the other with a dabbing rather than a brushing motion.

3

Continue until the stencil is filled in, then lift it carefully and move it on. It's a good idea to have a dry run before you begin and to clip the card so that you know exactly where to position it. If you use acetate stencils you can see the pattern below, but because they are flimsy they can be difficult to control. When you have finished, clean the stencil with paint thinner, and hang it up to dry. Coat areas of wear with polyurethane varnish.

Use stencilling for pattern on uneven walls where it's impractical to use wallpaper, or to decorate furniture or floors. The room above is striped with stencils in azure and plum on a creamy yellow ground, combining the colours which appear in the furnishings. These are defined by further stripes which terminate in tassels — a finishing touch impossible to achieve with wallpaper. The simple table on the right is given importance by the stylized floral stencil which forms a border round the central panel. Once again colours have been chosen to harmonize with existing furnishings so that the table blends with the overall scheme as well as being an attractive feature in its own right.

Compensate for the lack of architectural features by using stencils to add interest to a room. The modern room above has been furnished in traditional style, with period furniture, classic upholstery, an imposing window treatment and a mass of paintings and ornaments, but in the absence of a cornice something was needed to balance the valance. The solution was to stencil a border in shades of red to emphasize the russet used elsewhere in the room. The room below is equally plain, though quite different in style. Here interest is added in the shape of a false window frame which draws attention to the dormer, topped by a floral arrangement stencilled in a blue which complements that of the colour washed walls and floorboards.

Colour Washing

Colour washing is the most nostalgic, countrified finish in the decorator's current repertoire. Its soft unevenness of colours is reminiscent of faded old cottage walls in pinks, blues and ochres. Their look is the work of time and weather on traditional limewashed surfaces, coloured in crude powder colour which mellows beautifully as it ages. To imitate this indoors, instantly, you can use a variety of approaches.

One of the easiest to handle — and the most practical because it's hard wearing — is to brush a thinned tinted glaze loosely and not too evenly over a white base, and then to soften out the brushmarks with a brush, creating a cloudy effect.

Walls and window frame colour washed in apricot form a warm contrast to the cool lakeside scene outside.

Colour washing is a finish with simple, unpretentious charm rather than polished style. This suits smaller rooms with a quirky shape, low ceilings and odd windows. And it is also the ideal way to give a room a sunny, artless quality with a dash of country-style appeal.

The traditional method of colour washing is to use distemper, for which a recipe is given below. There are other methods of colour washing, however, which produce very satisfactory results. Washes of gouache (water-based artists' colour), with a dollop of latex for body, can be brushed over walls painted with a base coat of flat latex, for example, giving an excellent texture and filmy colour. Or, a less demanding alternative is the method used here, where a thinned standard glaze is brushed out and softened over an alkyd semigloss base.

Technique

There are several ways to achieve a colour-washed effect; here we used a translucent glaze made from 30 per cent scumble glaze, 50 per cent alkyd semigloss paint (we used aqua to suit the style of the bathroom) and 20 per cent paint thinner, applied over a base coat of white alkyd semigloss paint.

It's possible to use straightforward latex paint to create a colour wash provided it is used over a base coat of latex and that it is thinned with water to produce the required effect. Apply it with a wide (4 inch) wall brush, with random strokes (this is called cross-hatching) to vary the strength of colour and finish with transparent glaze.

Distemper is the material traditionally used for colour washing. It gives a delightfully subtle colour but its drawbacks are that it wears away and that it must be removed before you apply anything else on top. It is possible to use stabilising solution or diluted pva adhesive as a bonding coat first but the risk is that the weight will cause the stabiliser and distemper beneath to pull away from the wall. To make distemper, you will need 6½ pounds of whiting (mostly powdered chalk) available from speciality home improvement stores, 1lb of glue size, powder colour (artists' pigment or poster paint), cold water, a teaspoon and three buckets, two medium and one large, of hot water.

Make up the size as directed on the packet in one of the smaller buckets and leave until almost solid. Meanwhile half fill the second smaller bucket with water and pour in the whiting so that it rises above the surface. Leave to soak for an hour and stir well. Now dissolve some powder colour in cold water and add little by little to the whiting solution. Stir until evenly mixed. Next place the container of size inside a large bucket or tub of very hot water (over heat if possible) and wait until the size is runny. Pour the warm size into the whiting mix and stir thoroughly. The distemper should be a similar consistency to latex paint; if it is too thick, try warming it. You can add more water (you'll need to thin distemper for a colour wash) but too much will give an uneven effect. Distemper does not keep for more than a couple of days.

Equipment

For the translucent colour wash shown here you will need:
- white alkyd semigloss paint.
- a roller or brush.
- 30 per cent scumble, 50 per cent alkyd semigloss, 20 per cent paint thinner glaze.
- a paint bucket for the glaze.
- a large (4 inch) wall brush.

First apply a coat of white alkyd semigloss paint and allow to dry.

Apply the glaze, moving the brush in all directions to prevent the glaze from trickling down the wall. Brush out any obvious edges but leave some areas of background uncovered. Leave to dry overnight.

Repeat the process, this time covering the white areas for an attractively varied effect. In areas of hard wear, like the bathroom shown here, finish when dry with a protective coat of matt polyurethane varnish.

This close-up of the bathroom shows the broken colour produced by colour washing. It makes an ideal background for treatments such as stencilling – more interesting than a plain finish but less distracting than a patterned one.

Malachite Finish

Malachite is a fantasy finish which looks far more difficult to do than it really is, once you grasp the principle. It undoubtedly helps to look at examples of the real stone: malachite is usually striped in vivid greens, though variations exist. You might even follow the example of some professional decorators who collect small specimens of malachite, along with other types of mineral substances and natural materials, to give them inspiration and prevent their work from becoming a stylized formula. This treatment resembles oyster walnut grain, which can be simulated successfully using the same method, with shades of brown instead of green.

Plastic into precious stone: malachite is just one of the paint effects which imitate rocks and gemstones.

Malachite is one of the most valuable of the semi-precious stones. Its natural colour is a deep jade green with bluish overtones. To imitate this, most decorators use a glaze made from 70 per cent scumble glaze and 30 per cent paint thinner tinted with artists' oils in viridian over a green background, softening the effect with a badger brush or blender (see page 184). Here we chose to ignore nature and to concentrate on the 'striation' or texture of the rock. It's worth visiting a geological museum or gem stone store to examine a piece of cut malachite, as it helps if you have some idea of how the characteristic pattern is formed.

Technique

The basic tool in painting malachite treatments is actually a piece of roughly torn cardboard! Practise making the bold markings beforehand, softening the effect with a rag and brush to re-create the look of layers of radiating minerals under compression. A high polish, using varnish, completes the resemblance. Malachite might be overpowering on a large surface, but its jewel-like effect is gorgeous on this shelf surface, and is ideal for smaller items like frames, lamp bases, boxes and panels.

The medium used here is ordinary alkyd semigloss paint in an aqua shade to blend with the bathroom colour scheme, and the malachite finish has been applied to plain white laminate shelves, rubbed down with fine grade abrasive paper so paint will adhere and wiped clean with paint thinner. You'll need to experiment first to achieve an acceptable finish and a lot will depend on your ability to mimic the rock's veined appearance, but it's a treatment that can make even a modern plastic surface something to treasure.

Do's and Don'ts

DO ... rub down melamine or laminate so paint will adhere.

... use cardboard with an irregular edge to copy the striations of the rock.

... vary the direction of the pattern from time to time.

... protect the finish with polyurethane varnish to which a little white gloss or alkyd semigloss paint has been added to prevent yellowing.

DON'T ... forget to soften the background with a softening brush or a rag, to eliminate brushmarks.

... omit to renew the cardboard when it becomes soggy or clogged.

... work in too regular a way, or you will form stripes.

... use malachite on too large an area – it's best kept for ornaments and details.

Equipment

For this treatment you will need:
● white laminate or gloss-painted shelves, sanded so paint will adhere.
● a lint-free cloth.
● a paint tray.
● alkyd semigloss paint in the colour of your choice.
● a piece of cardboard (one torn from the fold of a tissue box is ideal).
● a 'fitch' (a small stubby brush – see page 184).
● gloss and matt finish polyurethane varnish.
● white gloss or alkyd semigloss paint.

1

First wipe the shelf clean with paint thinner. Pour some paint into the paint tray, fold the rag into a pad and dip it into the paint, removing the excess on the ribs of the tray. Daub it over the shelf to achieve an even distribution of colour. (This method eliminates brush marks.)

2

Take the piece of cardboard and drag it gently through the paint to create the striations characteristic of malachite, wiggling it gently from side to side as you go. Make sure that the edge of the cardboard is irregular to prevent straight lines.

3

Take the 'fitch' or stubby brush and place it firmly in the gaps between the swirls. Twist it until the bristles splay out to form tiny circles. Leave the finish to dry, then coat with one layer of gloss polyurethane varnish followed by another of matt, adding a touch of white gloss or alkyd semigloss paint to the varnish to prevent yellowing.

Romantic Nights

Duskily glowing as a damask rose, this romantic bedroom remains intimate, even cosy, despite lofty ceiling and windows. Transparent rose-mauve glaze dragged over ivory-painted walls makes a soft but vibrant background to the Victorian opulence of the huge, lace-covered brass bed, frilled glass shades and a plump buttoned velvet chair. The same colour, used full strength, underlines the strong horizontals of baseboard, picture rail and the delicate fuchsia stencilled border. More lavishness is provided by a tortoise-shelled mirror frame and spattered tops to mahogany-grained cabinets.

The 'strie' effect characteristic of dragging is created by a deep glaze brushed over a pale background which 'grins' through.

Dragging

Dragging requires a very steady hand!
In this technique, brush bristles are dragged
evenly down through a still-wet glaze to produce a
finely striped effect, accentuated when a coloured
glaze is applied over a much paler base coat.
Dragging gives a subtle, textured effect, hardly
visible at a distance, and yet rich enough to give
wall colours depth and softness. A dragged finish
has a somewhat formal look which looks best in
rooms with high ceilings and traditional
architectural details. The most technically
demanding treatment, dragging remains popular
because it makes such a flattering background to
fine furniture and pictures.

*Dragging has a formality which is ideally suited to
traditional room settings and furnishings.*

Dragging is deservedly popular because it forms a sympathetic background for furnishings and other paint treatments.

Technique

Like many techniques on wet glaze, dragging is easier if you have a partner. It is not a finish for complete novices to try: in addition to working on a wet glaze, it's important to keep the brush strokes as straight as possible. If you can't do this in one easy movement, work from the top of the wall to a point about two-thirds of the way down and then complete the section working from the baseboard up, easing the pressure as you approach the seam and gently feathering the stroke to join the two. (This movement also helps to avoid a heavy build-up of glaze at the base of the wall.) Vary the seams so that they don't coincide or they may form a distinct horizontal band across the wall. As you are removing – not applying – colour, remember to clean the brush every time you complete a strip, to maintain the same depth of finish. A special dragging brush is easiest to use, but you can substitute a paper-hanging brush or a large paint brush.

Choose a light background and a deeper tone than you actually want for the glaze, as the final effect will be considerably lighter. The base coat should consist of alkyd semigloss paint while the glaze is the regular 70 per cent scumble, 20 per cent alkyd semigloss, 10 per cent paint thinner mix, applied in bands. Don't attempt to press heavily on the brush in an effort to keep it straight. You will find it easier to maintain a consistent stroke if you run it lightly over the wall. Mark a faint guideline with a plumb bob and line near the corner where you intend to start and at intervals across it so that you don't go off at an angle. Finally, don't be discouraged if you find it impossible to avoid the odd wavy line – the point of this paint treatment is that it is a craft and it doesn't pretend to machine-made precision. If that's what you want, you can always buy wall-paper! It's a good idea to start on small pieces of furniture, like the wall cupboard shown in the stippled kitchen, and to progress to walls when you have mastered the technique.

Do's and Don'ts

DO ... keep a 'wet edge' – don't allow the glaze to harden.

... make sufficient glaze to cover an entire wall; if possible, a complete room.

... 'feather' any build-up of glaze at baseboard or ceiling level.

... stagger the seams if you are not dragging from top to bottom in one movement.

DON'T ... try to drag a top coat of latex paint; it dries far too quickly.

... apply the glaze in bands wider than 18 or 24 inches if working alone.

... forget to clean the brush regularly.

... break off or change batches of glaze in the middle of a wall.

Equipment

You will need:

● alkyd or latex semigloss paint for the base coat.

● a paint brush, or roller and paint tray, to apply it.

● deep tinted glaze (70 per cent scumble, 20 per cent alkyd semigloss, 10 per cent paint thinner) for dragging.

● a paint bucket.

● a wide (3 or 4 inch) paint brush for applying the glaze.

● a dragging, paper-hanging or wide paintbrush for dragging.

● plenty of rags and paint thinner for cleaning the brush.

1

Paint the wall with pale alkyd or latex semigloss paint (we used ivory for a delicate effect) and leave to dry. Then mix up the glaze in the paint bucket and apply it with a wide wall brush working from the top of the wall down in bands about 18 inches wide.

2

Take the dragging brush and with a light, steady movement, pull it through the glaze from top to bottom so that the bristles leave the faint 'strie' marking characteristic of the technique. Feather away any build-up of glaze at the baseboard and repeat.

3

Dragging makes an attractive background for more defined paint techniques such as stencilling. This fuchsia design is stuck down with masking tape and filled in with signwriters' paint applied with a stubby stencil brush. (For an explanation of stencilling, see pp. 136-141.)

Cissing

Cissing is the use of paint thinner to mottle a wet glaze — a type of negative spattering. Here it's used for 'fossilizing', a mock stone effect which aims to convey the colour and texture of stone and shells. Collect samples of porphyry, pebbles, rock and shell to give you an idea of the colours and striations of the natural material. Blend pink, beige, grey and oyster, or ivory, charcoal and grey-green for a realistic effect. Don't worry if the impact seems to fade as it dries; a coat of polyurethane varnish will bring it to life again.

The mottled effect of cissing is emphasized by the lightly dragged walls. The cissed table-tops, protected by clear varnish to which a little white alkyd paint has been added to prevent yellowing, draw together the major colours used in the room.

1

Clean, sand and prime the table-tops if necessary (see Basic Decorating Techniques pp. 58-61), apply two base coats of alkyd paint and leave to dry. Take the larger artists' brush, dip it into one batch of glaze and dot liberally over the surface. Clean the brush, then repeat with the second batch of glaze, still allowing some of the background to show through.

2

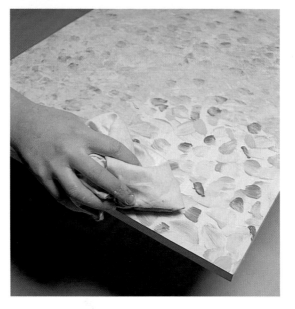

Shape the cloth into a pad and dab over the glaze to blend the two colours. You should now have a faintly marbled background.

3

Take the smaller brush and use it to spatter the paint thinner by knocking it against a piece of wood.

Wipe the brush and deepen the effect by dipping it into the third batch of glaze and flicking it over the surface.

Wet the sword liner or fine artists' brush and use to trace in faint vein markings for a realistic 'fossil' effect. Allow to dry, then finish with two coats of polyurethane varnish to which a little white alkyd paint has been added.

Technique

This treatment consists of daubing on patches of paint, ragging them together to soften the edges, and spattering with paint thinner. It's essential to carry it out on a horizontal surface or the paint thinner will form runs rather than circles. You'll need to protect the finish with varnish if it's subject to wear. Choose a heavy-duty polyurethane varnish for table-tops to resist ring marks; standard grade varnish is suitable for objects that are purely decorative.

Do's and Don'ts

DO ... choose horizontal surfaces for any treatment which involves spattering with paint thinner, to avoid streaking.
... select related colours.
... mottle the initial cissing thoroughly.
... protect the surface with polyurethane varnish.
DON'T ... attempt to cover large surfaces.
... use too large a brush or shake paint thinner over the surface without knocking on wood. The aim is to achieve a fine spattering of paint thinner for a delicately pitted look.
... rush the process.

Equipment

You will need:
● alkyd semigloss paint for the base coat.
● three batches of glaze mix in related colours made from 50 per cent scumble and 50 per cent alkyd semigloss paint.
● a paintbrush for the base coat.
● two artists' paint brushes (sable numbers 6 and 8).
● a sword liner brush (optional).
● lint-free cloth.
● paint thinner.
● a straight edge.
● varnish.
● a varnish brush or paint brush.

Tortoise-shelling

Tortoiseshell effects can be achieved with varnish or, as here, with glaze — an easier method as it is slower to dry and gives you more time to create the pattern.

Tortoiseshell is a rarity today, yet its glowing colours can transform an everyday tray or frame into treasure-trove.

Like many special effects, from marbling to malachite, it was developed as a substitute for expensive natural materials and the same *raison d'être* keeps the craft alive today. Although dark blue or green are occasionally used as a background (red is also a favourite for fantasy effects), it's usual to keep to the natural colours of polished tortoise-shell, where golden brown mingles with chestnut and black. It's a good idea to use a piece of natural tortoise-shell, or a picture of it, or to look at examples preserved in museums, for reference.

Choose a flat surface for your first attempt at this technique, as the colours tend to roll on curves, and confine it to small surfaces — decorative boxes, door panels, a tray or simple frame — as the effect can be overpowering used over a large area.

1

Prepare the surface, if necessary, and paint with two coats of sand colour alkyd semigloss. Allow to dry. Mix the first batch of glaze, using 20 percent paint thinner, 70 percent scumble and 10 percent raw sienna artists' oil in that order, to form an almost transparent glaze. Daub the glaze on with the fitch to cover the surface completely.

2

Dab the glaze with the cloth, bundled into a pad, to soften the effect.

3

Add more raw sienna to the glaze mix and daub in large, roughly oval patches, on top of the translucent glaze. Add burnt umber to darken the glaze and dab inside the areas painted with raw sienna to form smaller marks.

Add a little more burnt umber and some black to deepen the glaze still further and dab in the centre of these.

Take the badger softener and blur the tortoise-shell marks by pulling it across the surface towards you. Next, move it at right angles to your first movement before repeating the straight up and down action.

Finish by softening in different directions until the areas merge. If the first layer is still wet (but not if it's tacky), repeat the whole process for a more realistic effect.

Dip the stencil brush (or a similar stubby brush) into the glaze and finish by flicking tiny dots over the surface. Practise first on a piece of paper to make sure you don't spoil the effect. Allow to dry and varnish for protection and shine.

4

5

6

Technique

Remember to treat opposite rather than adjoining edges so that you don't smudge completed work. It's essential to use the right materials to achieve a realistic effect, so don't try to compromise with standard paint colours in place of artists' oils. You should find the colours you need in any art supply store and you only need a small quantity of each. Work patiently but with an eye on the overall effect; it's worth experimenting on something that's of little value until you get the hang of the technique.

Do's and Don'ts

DO ... assemble all the materials before you start to ensure a smooth workflow.

... soften well vertically and horizontally and finally in a random direction.

... repeat the process if the surface is still wet after the final softening.

DON'T ... try to make the three sets of marks too regular (keep to a roughly oval shape.

... be too hesitant about softening. The patches need to merge to produce the characteristic tortoise-shell effect.

... repeat the treatment if the glaze has become tacky.

Equipment

You will need:
● alkyd semigloss paint in a pale yellow (like that of a natural sponge) for the base coat.
● a paintbrush for applying it.
● scumble glaze.
● paint thinner.
● artists' oils in raw sienna, burnt umber and black.
● an artists' 'fitch' brush.
● a badger softener.
● a small stencil brush.
● lint-free cloth.
● clear varnish.

Fantasy effects add life and variety, transforming utilitarian objects into eye-catching features. A modicum of skill is required so they are not treatments for a beginner to attempt without practice. Because they are ornate – and labour-intensive – it's generally best to keep these complex effects to small objects and restricted areas, though the room below, with walls and ceiling clad in mock tortoise-shell, successfully breaks all the rules. Instead, use them to decorate mirrors, trays, table tops and shelves, and don't forget architectural features such as the fireplace and door frame. Attention to detail here makes an unexpected contribution to the decor in contrast to treatments designed to merge with the background.

Classic Elegance

Rooms for passing through rather than living in, like hallways, positively gain from dramatic contrasts and a sophisticated mix of textures. This once ordinary hall is transformed by the hard-edge look of glossy yellow walls and sharp white-on-black marbling of the woodwork. Painted floor squares, lightly veined, recall the marble and slate floors in stately homes and add dazzling lightness to a frequently underlit area. Painted marbling blends in with the hall's furnishings, while the mahogany-grained handrail and balusters add a note of restrained warmth.

Try your hand at the simple marbling which covers the plywood floor tiles before progressing to the more advanced black marbling technique displayed on the baseboards.

White Marbling

Marbling, or the simulation of various types of marble with paint and glazes, is the most challenging of all the decorative paint techniques if one is aiming at a faithful, eye-deceiving reproduction of specific marbles. Professional marblers and grainers — the two skills are usually combined — can reproduce as many as forty different types of marble from memory. However, it is quite possible to create a marbled effect which is attractive and elegant, without attempting trompe l'oeil accuracy. Work from a sample, if possible, and follow the technique described here faithfully, keeping the veined areas positive and using a softening brush to blur your lines.

This sumptuous marble floor is made from plywood tiles, painted and interspersed with black diamond-shape scraps.

Technique

Don't be put off by the fact that this is one of the more ambitious paint treatments. Even school-children often try their hand at marbling as a part of arts and crafts, and as long as you try to capture the spirit of marble, rather than slavishly reproducing its appearance, you shouldn't go far wrong. Remember that the veins run diagonally and that they go right across the rock — a point to consider even if you prefer fantasy marbling in bright or pastel colours to the naturalistic interpretation shown here.

White and grey marble are the easiest to live with, especially when used over a large area like the floor shown here. Deepen the colour — for practical reasons — when marbling floor tiles, and add a little white gloss paint to the varnish to prevent yellowing.

When preparing the ground, try to create a unified appearance, or divide the surface into a grid to simulate square tiles. A surface that's obviously made of bricks or planks will fight your attempts to 'marble-ise' it. Bear in mind that the real thing is both expensive and heavy, so it's rare to find marble used in large areas — except in palaces. Fill any cracks and rub down meticulously before you apply the base coat or flaws will show through the marble treatment, and consider laying plywood tiles like those shown here when treating a floor (for instructions on how to cut and lay see Basic Decorating Techniques, page 96). This has the added advantage that you can paint the squares individually rather than in situ, provided you keep in mind the flow of the design and the way the veins should run. Plain black scraps can be used to form the diamonds which traditionally intersect marble flooring.

Protect the finish with clear varnish to add gloss – floors will need a minimum of three coats of heavy-duty polyurethane. Don't skimp this step; marbling is a complex technique and there's little point in spending hours on achieving the finish if it wears away in weeks. Properly protected, a marble-effect floor should last for years, and when the varnish does show signs of wear it can be carefully rubbed down and resealed.

Do's and Don'ts

DO ... start by marbling small items.

... keep a piece or photograph of marble, or an example of marble paint treatment, for reference.

... ensure that 'veins' connect and run diagonally.

... protect the finish with varnish.

DON'T ... attempt a realistic finish on an inappropriate item.

... forget to soften the background.

... overdo the number of veins.

... try to marble-ise vertical surfaces.

Equipment

For simple marbling you will need:

● off-white alkyd semigloss paint for the base coat.

● a 2 to 3 inch paintbrush.

● 30 per cent scumble, 50 per cent bone-colour alkyd semigloss, 20 per cent paint thinner glaze.

● a paint bucket.

● raw sienna and black artists' oils.

● lint-free cloth.

● a sword liner or pointed artists' brush.

● a badger brush for softening.

● matt or semigloss polyurethane varnish (heavy-duty for floors).

● a varnish brush or clean paintbrush.

1

Sand, clean, prime and undercoat the surface if necessary, then apply one or two coats of solvent-based paint to provide a smooth, opaque finish. Clean the brush and apply the bone-colour glaze, then take the rag, folded into a neat pad, and dab it over the background to soften the effect.

2

Mix a little black artists' oil with the raw sienna to make a dark grey. Take the sword liner or pointed brush and draw veins diagonally across the surface, varying the thickness and direction slightly as you go. Put in 'branch lines' or cross the veins occasionally to mimic the natural appearance of marble. Next add more veins in raw sienna, but be careful not to overdo the effect.

3

Soften the marbling with a badger brush, taking care to preserve the outline of the veins. Allow to dry. Coat with several layers of matt or semigloss polyurethane varnish (heavy-duty if it's to protect floor tiles) to which a little white gloss or alkyd semigloss has been added.

Black Marbling

Long ago, in classical times, it occurred to craftsmen that a painted imitation was not only cheaper but often produced more satisfactory results — wood or plaster painted to look like marble was far easier to work with than weighty chunks of the real thing. Trompe l'oeil skills in marbling reached their peak in the nineteenth century; marbling, as practised by decorative painters today, tends more towards ornamental effect than ultra-realism. The dramatic marbling on a near-black base, as used for the woodwork in this hallway, requires more expertise, but the principle is the same — an inventive approach providing plenty of variety.

What at first sight appears to be a marble hall often turns out to be pure illusion, all done with paint.

Technique

The secret of successful black marbling is to create a convincing ground before you attempt to paint veins and highlights. Though its opulent effect is best suited to areas like the panel and door frame shown here, beginners may find it easier to practise on horizontal surfaces first.

Black marbling is a more complex technique than 'nubellato' and one best restricted to small areas. Once you are familiar with these techniques you can try your hand at green, ochre or rose marble, and of course fantasy decoration in pastels which simulates the texture, not the colour, of marble. In both cases it's wise to limit the number of veins and highlights you add or you will get an unnaturally busy effect.

Keep realistic forms of marbling for structural items, like floors and fireplaces, and for small decorative pieces as it can look inappropriate on furniture.

Equipment

You will need:
- black alkyd semigloss paint for the base coat.
- 60 per cent scumble, 20 per cent white alkyd semigloss, 20 per cent paint thinner glaze.
- a paint bucket.
- a wide (3 or 4 inch) wall brush.
- lint-free cloth.
- a badger softening brush.
- paint thinner.
- a small quantity of 60 per cent scumble, 20 per cent black alkyd semigloss, 20 per cent paint thinner glaze for veining.
- a sword liner or pointed artists' brush.
- matt or semigloss varnish plus a little white alkyd semigloss or gloss paint.
- a varnish brush or clean paintbrush.

The finished effect. Black marbling is a complex technique which involves a considerable amount of freehand work, so it's important to have a picture of the intended result by you, as well as in your mind's eye, before you start.

Prepare the area to be treated in the usual way and paint with two coats of black alkyd semigloss paint. Allow to dry. Mix up the batch of white-tinted glaze to the consistency of cream and daub it on with the wall brush. Allow the background to show in parts and don't attempt to treat more than one yard at a time.

Now rag over the surface with the cloth, spreading the white glaze so that it dapples the background. Keep the finish uneven for a variegated effect.

Soften the ragging with a badger brush so that the background becomes grey and blurred, but don't eliminate all the shadows. Dip a rag in paint thinner, take it in your other hand, and rag gently as you soften to remove excess white glaze.

At this point you should have a cloudy grey mottled background with dark areas to suggest veins and paler highlights.

Pick up your sword liner or pointed brush and dip into the black glaze mix. Draw in fine veins, following the lines of the shadowy ones formed by the background treatment.

Now soften the effect gently with the badger brush, following the line of the veins.

This is the sort of effect to aim for. The 'marble' is now criss-crossed by a complex roadway of black veins with intersections, by-ways and arterial routes.

Clean the brush and dip into the white glaze. Now add thick veins and patches of white to simulate the quartz which occurs in natural marble; they should be quite large for realism.

9

Take the badger brush and soften well until the white patches blend with the background.

10

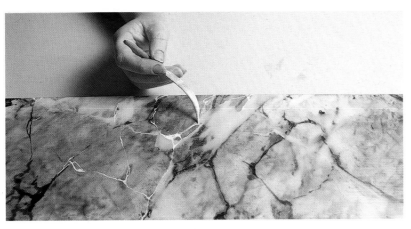

Finally, trace fine white veins on top to form highlights. Use the sword liner or a pointed brush for this, or a feather, which gives a very delicate effect.

11

Repeat the entire process until the surface is covered. Allow to dry and finish with a protective coat of varnish. (You will need several layers in areas of heavy wear like the door frame and stairway to protect the finish from knocks.)

12

A triumph of trompe l'oeil. This marble mantelpiece is surmounted by a second, painted version which lends importance to the original. A marble clad dado in the same nubellato finish is not only evidence of the fashionable classical revival but has a practical role in reducing the apparent height of the wall.

Marble' goes modern, used to decorate a small occasional table and matching mirror – a good choice for beginners because the area to be covered is small and the surfaces can be treated horizontally, minimizing the risk of runs. The deeper shade used here blends successfully with that of the classically white marbled floor.

Right: Marble is especially appropriate in a bathroom as this setting shows. It's not only the bath which has received the treatment; the walls and ceiling too are covered with a fantasy effect in a delicate combination of pink and blue on cream to match the colour of the handbasin and lavatory.

Wood-graining

After several decades of neglect, the old craft of graining is highly fashionable again — and deservedly so. A wood-grained treatment can dramatically transform the look of a room and give cupboards and bookcases made of fibreboard, chipboard and plywood the glamorous appeal of expensive hardwoods. Graining a room's woodwork, rather than simply painting it in flat colour, creates really classy textured surfaces which will offset the more elaborate wall finishes perfectly. This treatment is extra hard-wearing when properly varnished, and makes any room look more distinguished. Today's graining styles steer clear of the mustard-coloured 'varnished oak' so popular fifty years ago; instead they give softer, lighter and more subtly 'woody' effects, the smoky grey of limed oak currently top favourite. Mahogany graining has been used in this instance to give an ordinary soft wood handrail and newel post a rich and glossy hardwood look which contrasts well with the cool black and white marbling and gleaming yellow walls of this elegant hall.

1

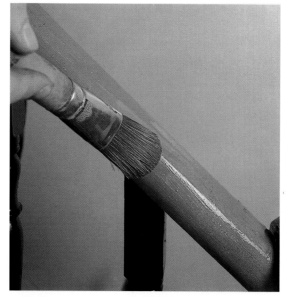

Prepare and fill the wood as explained above and finish with primer, undercoat and alkyd semigloss to give a smooth finish. Take the glaze and add a little burnt umber and burnt sienna until you have a rich, dark brown colour. Clean the paintbrush and apply the glaze. Allow to dry.

2

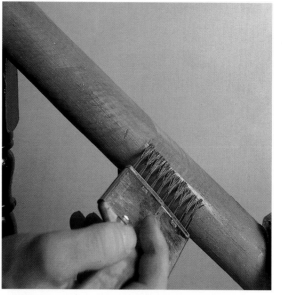

Now add more of the artists' oils to deepen the glaze still further (you won't need more than a yoghurt pot full) and apply with a graining brush in rings round the handrail.

3

At this half-way point the handrail should begin to take on the contours of natural wood. Don't worry if it still looks artificially hard at this stage.

Now soften the effect with the badger brush so that the rings are blurred. Leave the handrail until it is completely dry.

Darken the glaze still further with the burnt umber and burnt sienna. Apply a second layer with the graining brush in rings as before, remembering to soften well, and leave to dry.

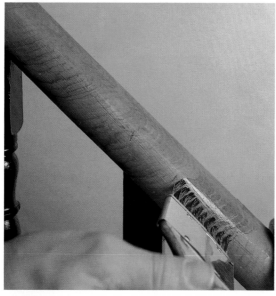

Finish with two coats of polyurethane varnish, rubbing down with fine abrasive paper between each, or use shellac to give a more natural warmth.

Technique

How can you turn chipboard into mahogany? Forget about veneer panels; the cheapest way is to paint it. Use a deep red-brown for the base, and over this a thin dark glaze applied with a graining brush or agitated with a steel or rubber comb to imitate the natural appearance of wood. It's essential to sand existing woodwork and to fill softwood and fibreboard, to mimic hardwood grain. Apply one coat of wood filler thinned to the consistency of cream. Allow to dry, then sand finely and clean before repeating the process. Next apply primer and undercoat, sanding between each, and finish with a base coat of reddish-brown alkyd semigloss that contains more than a hint of pink. Protect the finish with clear matt or satin varnish – gloss will highlight any flaws. A handrail may be finished with shellac, but don't use this for table-tops as you will find that water marks will be impossible to remove.

Equipment

You will need:
- wood filler, thinned to the consistency of cream.
- fine grade abrasive paper.
- primer.
- alkyd semigloss paint for the base coat in reddish-brown.
- a paintbrush (we used a 1 inch brush).
- 60 per cent scumble, 20 per cent alkyd semigloss (as for base coat) 20 per cent paint thinner glaze.
- burnt umber and burnt sienna artists' oils.
- a wood graining brush.
- a badger softening brush.
- shellac (button polish) or matt finish polyurethane varnish.
- a varnish brush or clean paintbrush.

Retro Chic

No need to raid Milan for Memphis flair when all you need is lots of bright, bold colour and plenty of nerve. The typically liquorice allsorts colour scheme is an effective disguise for dingy rooms and improvised or junky furniture. 'Striping' walls is a cinch with masking tape. Doodling colour on to a plainly painted floor is not only fun to do, but a swift reviver for dull boards – if well varnished to seal the squiggles in from wear and tear. One mismatched table leg provides a flash of Sotsass jokiness of the spot-the-deliberate-mistake variety.

Random, jazzy patterns like the ones which decorated the first laminates have a fifties look which is the height of retro chic. Anyone who can doodle can do them, with a limited budget and time to spare.

Masking

Painting a straight line freehand requires years of practice and a rock-steady hand. But thanks to masking tape it's possible even for a beginner to paint immaculate stripes like the ones shown here. Stripes make a bold statement in slick, smart dining rooms and little else in the way of decoration is needed to add to the effect. It's vitally important, though, that your measuring is accurate and the masking tape stuck down firmly in parallel lines. After this, creating the perfect stripe is simply a matter of brushing paint over the space between. For successful stripes, aim for solid colour. You may need to provide two coats over a dark, or contrasting base.

Custom-made 'planks' clock upturns the aqua and yellow horizontal stripes which set the pace in this room.

Sometimes you'll want a change from the soft, muted effect given by most paint treatments, which make such an ideal background for furniture and paintings. If you're short of possessions and want a bright room on a budget, consider a scheme like this where it's the decoration that makes the biggest impact. Reserve dramatic colour contrasts for areas which are used for a short time – the dining room is a perfect example – and choose a more restful combination of shades for rooms where there's more going on in competition with the decor (like the sitting room) or where you want relaxation rather than stimulation (like the bathroom).

Technique

Whichever style you choose, the most important technical point is to keep the stripes straight. A scheme like this demands absolute precision, so take care to find the true vertical for floor to ceiling stripes and check the horizontal with a spirit level if you want stripes running across the walls. Even if your guidelines are accurate you may have to adjust them if they look hopelessly out of true. This is usually because either the baseboard or moulding is not straight – it's best to use them as a guide rather than risk creating a scheme which looks lop-sided. Think twice before you introduce stripes in any form, paint or wallpaper, into an old house with irregular walls and sloping floors as it may be impossible to achieve a satisfactory result. Modern rooms with comparatively straight walls are best suited to strictly geometric schemes.

Start by preparing the walls, filling any cracks and sanding to obtain a fine finish. The base coat should be as immaculate as you can make it, so apply a thinned priming coat of semigloss latex (diluted with water) or eggshell (thinned with paint thinner) before applying two top coats, rubbing down between each. Next, mark out the stripes by measuring the distance from the ceiling in at least five places and joining the marks with chalk to form a guideline. Step back to check if the line looks straight, and adjust if necessary. Make sure that the lines are faint. Carefully run masking tape along the top and bottom edge of your stripe. The type that's used for paste-up is the best choice because it does least harm to the surface, but if you use ordinary masking tape, remove excess adhesive by sticking it to a towel or sheet several times before you apply it to the wall. Leave it on for as short a time as possible and use it only on shiny surfaces like semigloss, as it may damage the more absorbent flat finishes when you try to remove it.

Equipment

You will need:
- semigloss alkyd or latex paint for the base coats.
- the same variety of paint, in the colours of your choice, for the stripes. (Remember to allow sufficient paint to block out the base colour. If you are painting dark over light, you may be able to economize by buying small cans.)
- a wall brush or roller and paint tray for the base coat.
- a paintbrush of the appropriate size for painting the stripes. Choose a narrow (¾ or 1 inch) brush for thin stripes, a wider one (2 or 3 inches) for the broad version shown here.
- a spirit level.
- chalk.
- a straight edge.
- masking tape.

1

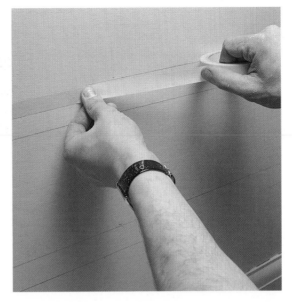

Once you are satisfied that your guidelines are level, apply strips of masking tape to butt up against the top and bottom edges of the stripe. Keep the tape taut to prevent it wrinkling and press it down hard to stop paint from seeping underneath.

2

Now paint the gap between the two lengths of tape. Allow to dry and repeat if necessary to achieve the correct intensity of colour.

3

As soon as the paint is touch-dry, remove the tape with a steady downward action. Stop immediately if the paint begins to peel away and cut round this area with a safety blade. As long as the damage is limited, it can be touched in later.

Flicking and spattering in the Jackson Pollock style (above) requires bright colours, a paint consistency thick enough to make bold doodles where it lands, and a bit of nerve – to begin with – because the procedure is so contrary to the usual practice. Experiment with different types of brushes, with latex paint both slightly thinned and full strength, and from varying distances (far right). The controlled use of spattering makes an excellent disguise for smaller surfaces like tables and fireplace surrounds, and by choosing colours that key into your room scheme (right) you can make sure that they merge unobtrusively with your other furnishings.

Moody Blues

Rolling a small bolster of rags up a freshly glazed wall creates an elegant, wavy effect, like old-fashioned watered silk. A sky blue glaze rag-rolled is luminous and refreshing in this sophisticated living room, with its cool Scandinavian-style white drapes and dark polished wood floor. Stencils based on a stylized lotus flower design discreetly underline the classic shapes of a painted table and pedestal. No pictures, but instead the twirling shapes of painted fans on a modern japanned screen.

Formal rag rolling gives this room elegance, while the clever use of colour and stencils transforms the screen, pedestal and coffee table into pieces which are both attractive and linked to the general scheme.

Rag-rolling

A room that has a period feel, with relatively high ceilings, symmetrically placed windows, elegant details such as plaster cornices, panelled doors, and generous mouldings round doors and windows, is a perfect candidate for the subtly formal-looking treatment of old fashioned rag rolling. Unlike simple ragging which gives soft all-over patterning, rag rolling looks remarkably like watered silk. The effect is feminine with a flavour of the eighteenth century and looks best in the muted pastel colours popular at that time. Greyish pinks, washed-out yellows, cloudy sky-blues or light greens are good rag rolling colours. For a less feminine air, choose pearl grey, or buff.

Rag rolling in contrasting colours creates a warm background which suits the rich style of this setting.

Technique

Rag rolling is a more precise technique than simple ragging. The aim is to produce a moiré, or watered silk pattern, which needs to be a) straight and b) regular rather than patchy. Because it is carried out on a wet glaze you won't have time to adjust your technique halfway through. You must complete a whole wall (and preferably an entire room) at a time, using the same batch of glaze to produce consistent results. The process is very much easier if you can co-opt someone to help, so that as one applies the glaze, the other follows with the rags. If you need – or prefer – to work alone, it's essential to practise on the back of a length of wallpaper, or on a scrap of lining paper, before you begin. Don't lay the paper on the floor; stick it to the wall with adhesive gum so that you can experience the problems of applying the glaze and manipulating the rags. Use a plumb bob and line to establish the vertical, as it's only too easy to veer to one side or the other – and it looks all too obvious with a directional design like this.

Make sure you have several rag 'sausages' made from the same material and the same size (4 to 6 inches wide) before you start. You'll have to discard the rags as they become clogged and you won't have time to search for more once you have applied the glaze. Traditionally, rag rolling is carried out working from the bottom of the wall upwards but you may find it easier to work from the top down. Remember, though, that gravity will cause the glaze itself to move down, and that you'll have to allow for a greater build-up of paint near the baseboard. Keep a cloth damped with paint thinner at hand to cope with heavy patches and use a

Paint the walls with alkyd semigloss or a similar solvent-based paint and allow to dry, then take the plumb bob and line to establish the vertical in several places (see Basic Decorating Techniques p.36). Now you are ready for rag rolling.

Mix up the glaze in a paint bucket and brush on to the wall in a strip about an arm's width across. Apply the glaze evenly to avoid patchiness.

Take your rag 'sausage' and run it from bottom to top (or top to bottom if you prefer) of the wall. Repeat, with a marginal overlap, until you reach the edge of the glazed area, then apply the next strip of glaze and start again. Continue in this way until the wall is complete, making sure that the edges of the glazed strips merge but avoiding a heavy overlap.

Cool blue colour complements the watered silk effect produced by classic rag rolling. It creates a soft background for the blend of simple modern shapes and decorated furniture which distinguishes this living room.

1

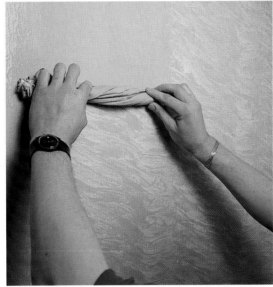

2

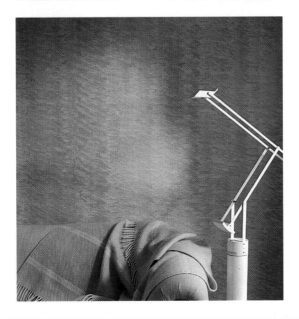

3

small brush to feather in as necessary. Alternatively, make a virtue of necessity and paint a 'ribbon' of darker glaze at the ceiling and baseboard edge.

Do's and Don'ts

DO ... use pastels to minimize patchiness.
... check the vertical to keep the pattern straight.
... make sufficient glaze to cover an entire wall.
... practise before you begin.
DON'T ... be tempted to use latex paint rather than glaze when rag rolling. It can look very pretty but dries so fast that it is best left to the professionals.
... run out of rags or glaze half-way through.
... change the type of rags you use.
... panic. Work methodically and dab off excess glaze with a rag soaked in paint thinner. Remember that rag rolling is not supposed to look as if it has been done by a machine — and that you can erase the effect with a coat of alkyd semigloss paint if you want to start again.

Equipment

You will need:
- alkyd or similar solvent-based paint for the base coat.
- a roller or paintbrush for applying it.
- a plumb bob and line and a pencil for marking the vertical.
- a bunch of lint-free rags rolled into a sausage shape. (This should be slightly tighter than for the ragging technique on p.108).
- glaze/paint/paint thinner mix (as described on p.108).
- a paint bucket.
- a 3 or 4 inch paint brush.
- an artist's paint brush for feathering in edges.
- a cloth wrung out in paint thinner to remove drips and patches.

Decorated Furniture

Why stop at the walls? All the treatments described in this section look equally effective on furniture. Decorating a piece of furniture can turn the mundane — a chipboard cupboard or an undistinguished chair — into something that's unique. Even if you don't achieve a work of art on William Morris lines you'll have the satisfaction that at the very least it complements your colour scheme. Use the softer treatments, like dragging or sponging, as a background for detailed designs and for larger pieces. Keep elaborate techniques for small areas so that they don't overwhelm the room. Protect the completed work with varnish so that the finish resists wear.

Wicker into work of art: this bedroom chair is decorated with a freehand design repeated on the matching cushion.

The simplest furniture — whether an old and junky piece or a new but unassuming one — gains immediate distinction and a dressed-up look when adorned with stencilled patterns (above) or designs painted freehand (centre and far left). Brighten up bamboo (left), that's past its best with the technique described on page 134 but remember that any object that's used and moved around and handled — as most furniture is — needs to be painted to the highest standards. A good paint job ages gracefully, even gaining in appeal when the paint begins to wear a little thin, whereas, a quick paint facelift merely looks shabby and chipped with time.

Murals & Trompe l'oeil

Trompe l'oeil is a French expression meaning 'fool the eye'. Like a brilliant conjuring trick, this technique elicits admiring incredulity once the truth is discovered, an amused – 'Well, I never!' reaction. It demands a high degree of skill and for the amateur decorative painter, the sort of trompe l'oeil subject which is easiest to pull off is the minutely observed still life of familiar objects. You could spice up the plain doors of a cupboard, with its ideal contents: leather-bound books, for example, or precious porcelain. On a larger scale, for more competent painters, there is trompe l'oeil of the architectural variety – painted pillars and doorways with views beyond.

The importance of shading to give perspective to trompe l'oeil is shown in this impressive 'staircase'.

Combine fact with fantasy to fool the eye! Trompe l'oeil makes it difficult to distinguish truth from illusion as these settings, which mingle straightforward architectural elements with surrealism, show. Trompe l'oeil can expand to become a mural or simply decorate an uninteresting corner. Almost any paint can be used, from odds and ends of latex colours tinted with stainers or intermixed, to the more expensive acrylic artists' colours — popular with the professionals because they dry so quickly. Washes and glazes or thinned colours tend to look more satisfactory than bright, opaque, full-strength colour because the softer tones blend together more harmoniously. But there are no hard and fast rules; the important thing is to have the confidence to get the project off the ground. Once results begin to show, your own creative excitement — and the enthusiasm of interested onlookers — will encourage you to see it through.

Almost any paints can be used for murals and trompe l'oeil, from odds and ends of latex colours tinted with stainers or intermixed, to the more expensive acrylic artists' colours – popular with the professionals because they dry so quickly. Washes and glazes or thinned colours tend to look more satisfactory than bright, opaque, full-strength colour because the softer tones blend together more harmoniously. But there are no hard and fast rules; the important thing is to have the confidence to get the project off the ground. Once results begin to show, your own creative excitement – and the enthusiasm of interested onlookers – will encourage you to see it through. Once you have gained confidence, you will be able to progress to more ambitious projects.

Murals

Murals are wall paintings; the painted wall itself is treated as a 'picture'. The simplest designs are the easiest to enlarge and to paint so opt for a stylized picture-book effect rather than going for naturalism, and choose an example to copy which contains large, clearly separated blocks of colour, even if you want the mural to represent a landscape or a flower garden. On the other hand, it's best to avoid very precise geometrics which demand absolute accuracy – difficult to achieve when painting freehand so use stencils for these instead. The ideal place for an amateur to try out a mural idea is in a small child's room. A child's world is fuelled by fantasy, and any reasonably competent person can transpose favourite storybook characters – say, Donald Duck or Puss-in-Boots – to a larger scale, using the illustrations as a model. Don't be afraid to introduce personal touches; a painting of the child or family, friends or pets will be magically rewarding, even if the portraits mightn't quite measure up to the standards of the National Gallery.

Once you have chosen your design, enlarge it on a photocopier, if necessary, and divide it into squares measuring 2 inches or so. Now copy this grid on to the wall, scaling the design to the size you require. The wall should be carefully prepared and painted with a base coat in the colour of your choice. Thorough preparation is especially important here as this is one wall you most certainly won't want to redecorate every year!

Mark out the perimeter of the design using chalk or soft pencil, establishing vertical lines with a plumb line and bob and checking horizontals with a spirit level to ensure accuracy. Snap chalked lines against the wall to fill in the interior of the grid.

Copy one section at a time on to the wall, following the lines shown in each block on your original design. When the outline is complete, step back and check that it's accurate. Paint the mural one colour, not one section, at a time, using the appropriate size of brush (an artists' brush for fine detail, a small paintbrush for filling in) working from the top down. Allow each colour to dry before you apply the next to prevent smudging. It's cheaper to use straightforward latex or alkyd paint, particularly if you want to use up odd lots of paint or buy small sample cans, but choose acrylic artists' colours for extra brilliance. When the mural is completely dry, rub out the guidelines with a damp cloth. If you feel it needs more emphasis, outline the design with a standard felt tip pen. Finish by sealing with matt effect polyurethane varnish.

Trompe l'oeil

Can't afford to replace a cornice or add an architrave? Then paint them in, following the time-honoured technique of trompe l'oeil. As this is an effect which depends on realism,

If panelling's too pricey or you can't afford a fireplace, paint them, following the time-honoured technique of trompe l'oeil. Skilled artists might attempt the exotic dining room far left; simpler projects include the details which decorate the wall above the cooktop, top right.

it's not for complete beginners. Unless you are artistically gifted, it's best to keep either to simple details or to aim for a light-hearted effect, using the same technique employed to create a mural.

If you are planning to imitate architectural features, you might try stencilling the outline for accuracy before softening the effect with paint and glaze. Remember the importance of shading to give perspective, and use stippling or sponging to make the design blend with the background.

If creating a convincingly realistic effect is beyond your artistic abilities, concentrate on witty designs which will brighten up a dull corner and provide an interesting talking point.

Specialist Equipment

Most special finishes require special brushes, which are available from trade suppliers. Always buy the best — the difference in performance is enormous. Twirl new brushes to expose loose hairs and remove them. Always wash brushes thoroughly after use in a commercial cleaner. When not in use, store brushes flat with the bristles wrapped in brown paper, newspaper or foil.

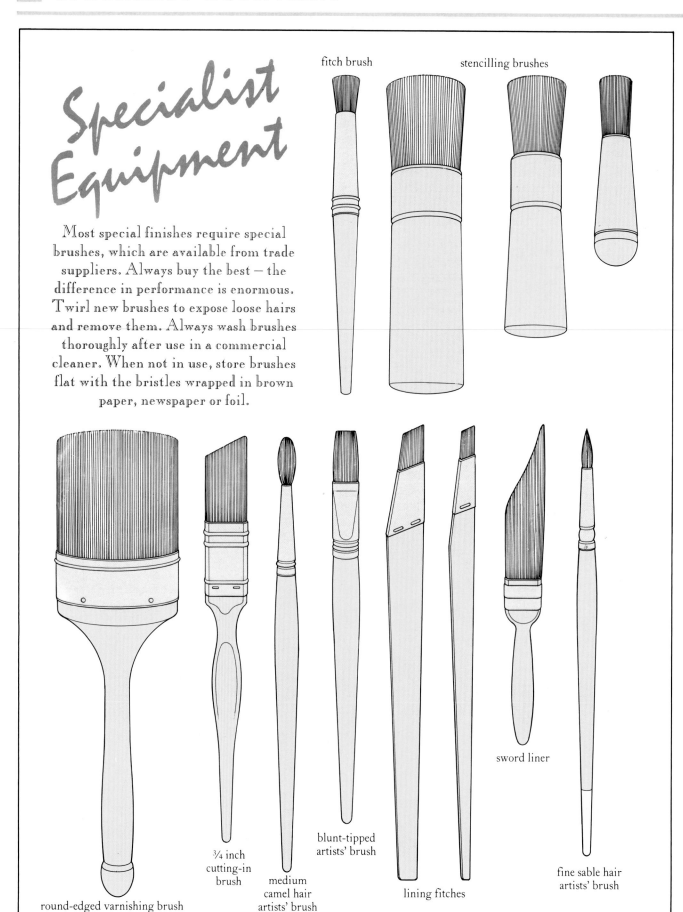

fitch brush

stencilling brushes

round-edged varnishing brush

¾ inch cutting-in brush

medium camel hair artists' brush

blunt-tipped artists' brush

lining fitches

sword liner

fine sable hair artists' brush

flogger, or dragging brush

graining brush

dusting brush

badger hair softening brush

overgrainer

mottler

stippling brush

Glossary

aluminium primer Water-resistant liquid used to seal and prime a surface before a topcoat is applied.

antiquing see **colour rubbing**

bambooing A technique for painting circular-sectioned wood to imitate the ring joints and grain of bamboo.

blowtorch A gas- or paraffin-fuelled torch giving an intense naked flame used to strip paint and varnish.

chipboard Rigid sheet material made from compressed and bonded wood chips.

cissing A mottled paint finish created by overlaying coloured glazes and partially lifting the colour with a solvent.

claw hammer A hammer with a flat striking face and two heavy prongs for levering.

cold cure varnish A high-gloss floor sealant prepared by mixing two specially formulated components.

colour rubbing A technique for simulating an aging paint surface by rubbing a partly dry glaze layer.

colour washing A technique for creating a hazy, translucent paint finish by applying a thinned layer of paint over a basecoat of plain colour.

combing A technique of creating a decorative paint finish by running a comb through wet paint or glaze applied over a plain-coloured ground.

cornice Ornamental moulding fitted to the angle between wall and ceiling. Made of plastic, wood or plastic resin.

countersinking The method of recessing a screw-head or bolt so it lies flush with a surface.

coving Plain moulding fitted to the angle between wall and ceiling, made of gypsum or wood.

cross peen hammer A hammer with a flat striking surface and ball-shaped end to the head.

cushioned vinyl Sheet flooring made of vinyl with an aerated foam layer over the backing which provides extra warmth, comfort and resilience.

distemper Paint consisting of pigment and whiting suspended in glue size; it dries with a chalky, matt surface.

dragging A technique for creating a strie-effect paint finish by pulling the bristles of a brush through a wet glaze layer.

enamel Solvent-based paint which dries to a hard, shiny finish, used especially for detailing and decorative work.

filler A compound in powder or paste form for filling cracks and cavities, in different types formulated to work on wood, plaster or stone.

flat oil paint A solvent-based paint which dries with a matt finish.

flicking A technique of creating a decorative paint finish by flicking random dots and runs of paint on to a plain-coloured ground and sealing the finish to fix it.

flock Wallcovering with a raised, velvety pattern made by compressing short textile fibres into an adhesive base laid on paper.

gloss paint Solvent-based paint which dries to a resistant, glossy finish.

graining see **wood graining**

grout A waterproof compound used to fill gaps between tiles or bricks.

hardboard A thin sheet material made of compressed wood pulp.

lacquer Solvent-based paint or varnish formulated to dry to a high-gloss finish.

laminate Hard plastic sheet material used as a washable facing layer on wood furniture, board etc.

latex Water-based paint of fluid consistency.

lining paper A thin wallcovering designed to provide a smooth ground for wallpaper or paint.

malachite A paint finish imitating the green-blue surface of the semi-precious stone, malachite.

marbling A decorative paint finish imitating the texture of marble, created by painting, dabbing and blending various colours.

melamine A sprayed plastic finish resembling laminate.

mosaic flooring Wood flooring laid from solid or veneered wooden panels usually arranged in a basketweave pattern.

non-drip paint Paint with a gel-like consistency which does not drip from a brush or roller but spreads easily on a surface.

paint remover A solvent designed to soften an existing paint layer.

parquet Wood flooring consisting of blocks fitted together in a regular interlocking pattern.

plasterboard Construction material consisting of a thickness of plaster compressed between outer layers of a fibrous board.

plywood Rigid sheet material made of thin layers of wood glued together. The grain in each layer runs crosswise over the previous one.

polyurethane varnish Synthetic liquid sealant available in matt, gloss or satin finishes.

pva (polyvinyl acetate) A plastic resin preparation in semi-liquid form used as an adhesive or sealant.

quarry tiles Small floor tiles made of unglazed ceramic.

ragging A painting technique for creating a textured effect by using rags to apply or remove paint or glaze.

rag rolling A technique which creates a regular 'watermark' pattern effect by rolling rags across a layer of wet glaze laid over a dry paint layer.

relief wallcovering A general term for wallcoverings with a raised design formed by embossing or chemical treatment.

shavehook A stripping tool with a triangular or combined straight and curved blade.

shellac A liquid varnish and sealant made from a natural resin.

silicon carbide paper Water-resistant paper with an abrasive coating, which can be used wet or dry to smooth down a rough surface.

size Thinned glue preparation dissolved in water, used as an adhesive, binding agent or sealant.

solvent A liquid preparation capable of dissolving an oily or resinous paint or varnish.

solvent-based paint Paint consisting of pigment suspended in oil or resin, which can be diluted or dispersed with a chemical solvent.

spattering A technique for creating a decorative paint finish consisting of a shower of fine dots of colour on a plain-coloured ground, by tapping, flicking or shaking a loaded paintbrush over the surface.

sponging A painting technique for creating a delicately coloured, cloudy effect by applying layers of paint with a sponge.

stencilling A technique of painting repeating motifs by working paint into cutout card shapes placed over a flat surface.

stippling A technique of creating a decorative paint finish by dabbing a stiff brush or sponge into wet glaze applied over a dry paint layer.

thixotropic The quality of a gel-like substance which becomes more fluid when agitated or spread, such as a non-drip paint.

tongue and groove A method of joining wood sections or tiles in which a protruding tongue on one section fits a grooved slot in another.

tortoiseshell A decorative paint finish in which dark-colored glazes are overlaid and patterned to imitate the surface coloring of natural tortoiseshell.

trompe l'oeil (deceive the eye) A painted image contrived to appear realistic and three-dimensional though actually flat.

undercoat Matt-finish paint designed to form a non-porous base layer for finishing coats. Also called primer.

vinyl A term used of products made with or consisting of vinyl resin which provides a tough plasticized texture; used for paint, wallcoverings, floorcoverings.

vinegar graining A textured grain effect applied over a plain ground by working into a partly dry coloured vinegar glaze using a rag, comb, fingerprints etc.

water-based paint In practical terms, a paint which can be diluted with or dispersed in water.

wood filler A paste-like compound used to fill holes in wood, which after drying will flex with any movement in the wood.

wood graining A technique of using paint and varnish to imitate a wood grain effect on a grainless surface.

wood stain Transparent liquid colouring which soaks into and colours wood.

wood strip Wood flooring laid from strips of solid hardwood or veneered softwood.

Index

Acknowledgments

Special photography: Bruce Hemmings
Stylist: Susie Knight
Paint finishes: Sally Kenny, assisted by Keith Padmore
and Andy Knight
Illustrations: Hayward Art Group

Odeon Style · 104
Rug from Helen Yardley,
3-5 Hardwidge St, London SE1.
Grey chairs and vases from Practical
Styling, 18 St Giles High St,
London WC1. Tables from
Conran, 77 Fulham Road, London
SW1. Blinds by Luxaflex. Wooden
block flooring from Texas
Homecare.

Country Style · 114
Apricot bedlinen and towels by Next
Interiors (local branches all over
G.B.). Antique bedlinen and
pillowcases from Lunn Antiques,
New Kings Rd, London SW6. Rag
rugs from Designers Guild,
277 Kings Rd, London SW3.

Rural Retreat · 124
Antique furniture from Phelps,
133 St Margarets Rd,
Twickenham, Middx. Flower motif
and mottled vases and plates from
Designers Guild (as before).

Border Country · 131
Fabric, wallpaper and soft throw
from Next Interiors (as before).
Chaise longue from Conran (as
before). Blue vases and bowl from
Designers Guild (as before). Carpet
from Marks and Spencer.

Water Colours · 137
Bath and basin and taps from Pipe
Dreams, 105 Regents Park Rd,

London NW1. Towels and tiles
from Next Interiors (as before).
Vases from Designers Guild (as
before). Bathroom accessories from
Conran (as before) and branches of
Boots.

Romantic Nights · 146
Curtain fabric and cushions from
Laura Ashley (branches all over
U.K.). Bedspread and cushions
(lace) from Lunn Antiques (as
before). Bedside lights from
Christopher Wray's Lighting
Emporium, New Kings Rd,
London SW6.

Classic Elegance · 157
Cachepot from General Trading
Store, 144 Sloane St, London SW1.

Retro Chic · 169
Blinds by Luxaflex. Vases by
Conran (as before). Lamp from
London Lighting, 135 Fulham Rd,
London SW6. Bowl and pedestal
from Practical Styling (as before).

Moody Blues · 174
Stencilled furniture from Coleen
Berry, 8 Rosehill Rd, London
SW18. Dhurrie rug from Mary
Fox-Linton, 249 Fulham Rd,
London SW6. Tizio lamp from
London Lighting (as before).

*All paints kindly supplied by Crown
Paints from the Colour Cue
Collection.*

The publishers wish to thank the following
organisations and individuals for their kind
permission to reproduce the photographs in this
book:

Peter Aaron/ESTO 56-57, 84-85 top; Jan
Baldwin/Good Housekeeping Magazine 35 top,
107 below; Bill Batten/The World of Interiors
70, 84 top left; David Brittain/Good
Housekeeping Magazine 182 top right; Michael
Boys 1, 27 below, 28 left, 84 below left, 100
below, 140 top, 148 left, 182 top left; Christian
Braud 6, 8-9, 68 top left; Carla de Benedetti
6-7; Camera Press 16-17, 42, 48 below centre,
48 below right, 61, 63, 68-69 top, 69 below, 72
right, 75 below, 94 below right, 102 left, 106,
107 top, 112, 126, 164 below, 173; Gary
Chowitz/EWA 100 top; Crown Plus Two
Paints 103 top right; Cover Plus Paints/F. W.
Woolworth 26 top right, 68 below centre, 118
below; Dragons of Walton Street 178-179;
Michael Dunne/EWA 26 below left, 48 below
left, 154-155 top, 181 below right; Andreas von
Einsiedel/EWA 76 left; Colin Failes 182
below right, 183; Elliot Fine Photography 34
below right; Roberta Frateschi 7 top right, 44,
48-49 top, 119; Bruce Hemmings/Orbis 2-3,
103 below right, 104, 105, 108, 109, 110, 111,
113, 114, 115, 117, 120, 121, 122, 123, 124,
125, 127, 128, 129, 130, 131, 134, 135, 136,
137, 138, 139, 143, 144, 145, 146, 147, 149,
150, 151, 152, 153, 156, 157, 158, 159, 161,
162, 163, 166, 167, 168, 169, 170, 171, 174,
175, 177, 178 left, 179 below right; Graham
Henderson/EWA 34 below left; Frank
Herholdt/EWA 154 left, 155 below left; Mark
Hornak/Angelo Hornak 160; The House of
MayFair – Satin Style 84 below centre; R.
Greg Hursley 22 top; Robert Hyett/EWA 96
top; ICI Dulux/Colour Collection and
Matchmaker ranges 18, 23 top, 64, 68 below
left and right, 72 left, 74 below left, 97; Iris
Ceramica s.p.a. 42-43; Lucinda Lambton/
ARCAID 35 below; Leland Y. Lee/The Lee
Side Inc. 34 top right, 172 top; Tom Leighton/
Good Housekeeping Magazine 74 below right;
David Lloyd/EWA 27 top; Neil Lorimer/
EWA 85 below, 94 below left; Maison de
Marie Claire/S. Belmont 102-103; /Durand
76-77; /Patau/Comte 132, 133 below, 182
below left; /Rozes/C. Hirscl Marie 94 below
centre; James Mortimer/The World of Interiors
74 top left; Next Interiors 7 below right, 15,
54-55, 118 top; Michael Nicholson/EWA
(Design: Richard Holley) 154 below right;
Oakleaf Reproductions Ltd. 34 top left; Peter
Paige Photography 84 below right; Hugh
Palmer/Good Housekeeping Magazine 73;
Spike Powell/EWA (Design: Silvy Schofield)
8, 26 top left, 26 below right, (Design:
Katherine and James Taylor) 95 below left,
(Design: Dagny Duckett) 179 top right; PWA
International/Living Magazine 74 below centre,
83, 94 top left; Malcolm Robertson/Good
Housekeeping Magazine 48 top left; B. C.
Sanitan 165; Philip Sayes/The World of
Interiors 141 top; Fritz von der Schulenburg
133 top, 141 below, 142, 164 top, 180 left, 181
top right; Richard Stanley Smith for Landseer
Property Corporation 180-181; Tim Street-
Porter/EWA 50, 51; Syndication International
4, 28-9, 34 below centre, 74-75 top, 116, 172
below, 176; Jerry Tubby/EWA 49 below left;
Peter Woloszynski/The World of Interiors 56
left;